THE AUSTRALIAN
Women's Weekly
cheat's cakes

Buy the cake then decorate it – no-stress birthday cakes for kids

BAUER

MEDIA GROUP

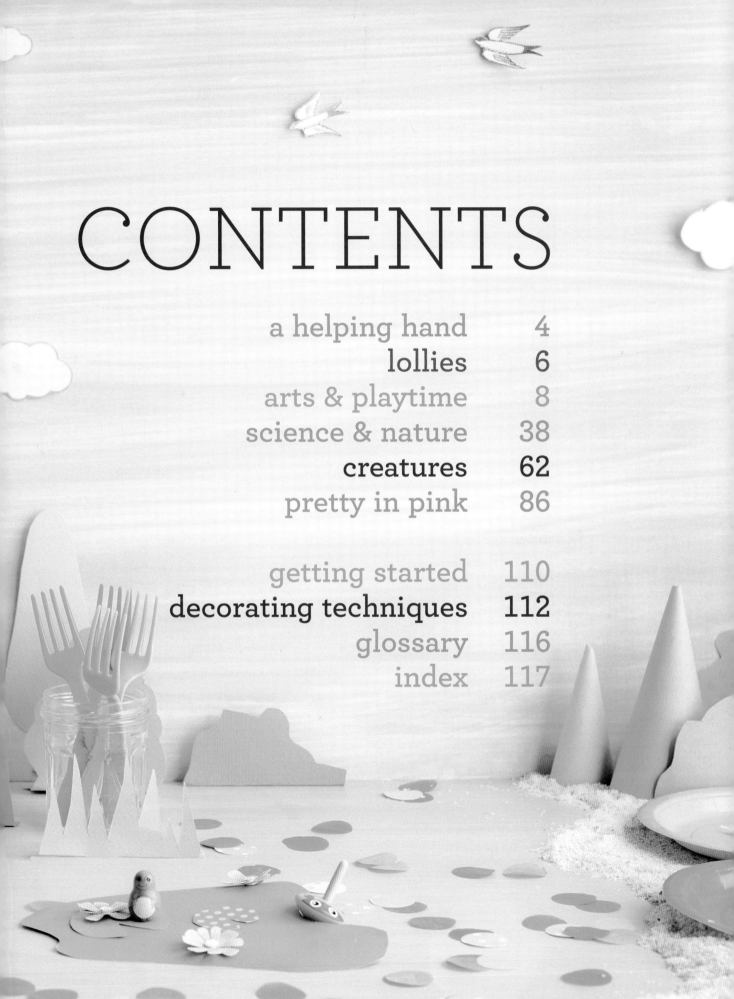

CONTENTS

a helping hand

The Australian Women's Weekly first started publishing recipes for kids' birthday cakes way back in the 1950s, and we soon became famous for them. Since that time we've produced many different birthday cakes, which have featured in both the magazine and The Weekly's cookbooks.

Today, we are finding people's lives, and that includes our own, are becoming busier, and sometimes the thought of making a cake from scratch can be overwhelming – not so much because we can't do it, but because we are already tired from our busy days, and really, no matter how much we love our kids, we just don't want to spend our 'down-time' weighing, measuring, beating and waiting for the oven to heat up.

So, we have created this book full of ideas on how to, not so much cheat, but to use the fantastic products available from supermarkets to help us make fun and fabulous birthday cakes that every kid will love.

This book is packed with clever and creative designs that will turn basic store-bought cakes and baked goods into delightful works of art. Anyone can create these cakes at home – just about everything is available from the major supermarkets. These shortcuts will help you whip up the perfect birthday cake without, mostly, turning on the oven or greasing a cake pan.

The cake designs that the Test Kitchen staff came up with are amazing – they are minimum fuss with maximum impact. This collection has a cake for everyone, from pretty cakes for girls who love pink, to Egyptian mummy cupcakes, a road crew cake and cakes for budding entomologists; all these cakes are sure to impress critical kids.

The supermarket is a treasure trove of ready-made ingredients for busy people. The cakes in this book are created using baked goods that you can purchase from the supermarket or bakery – square and round cakes, doughnuts, cupcakes, jam rolls, lamingtons, muffins and more.

Once you have decided on the cake, it's time to jazz it up. The confectionery and baking aisles are the perfect places to find everything you need. Lollies and pre-made frostings and icings, sprinkles, chocolate buttons and sugar decorations are all available and in even more variety than ever before.

A picture is worth a thousand words, and the fantastic pictures in this book show how the finished cake should look, making it simple to see and decorate your chosen masterpiece. By following the simple instructions, you can see exactly how to use these handy store-bought items to create a cake that makes everyone say 'wow'. For example, to see what you can do with different coloured jube lollies, turn to the wildfire flower cake on page 100. Simply by cutting the jubes, and carefully arranging them, we have turned a basic store-bought slab cake into a magical floral mosaic.

To make the most of these 'cheat's' cakes, read through the recipe before starting your shopping list – some of the cakes

need to set or freeze overnight; you need to know when you are going to decorate the cake, and how much time it will take. Decorating some of these cakes is fiddly work, but the end result is worth it – just take your time. Regardless of whether the cake looks picture perfect, or frantically thrown together, they will all bring a smile to the face of your child and the party goers.

At the back of the book there is a heap of information on how to ice cake pops, melt chocolate, make butter cream and ganache, and how to cover a cake board, if you want to cover your own. You can buy cake boards from cake decorating shops, the kitchen part of major department shops and, of course, online. Cake boards are great, as they make transporting the cake so much easier.

There is nothing as special as seeing your child's face light up when you bring out an Australian Women's Weekly birthday cake, but sometimes we just run out of time. This book of cheat's birthday cakes is the perfect tool for busy mums and dads.

LOLLIPOPS

MILK BOTTLES

MONSTER 5'S
ORANGE SPRINKLES

MUSK STICKS

ICING FLOWERS

MINI MERINGUES

MINI MALLOWS

RAINBOW LACES

FRUIT AND
COLA WHEELS

STARMIX
HEART
LOLLIES

MINI M&M'S

CELEBRATION 5'S
YELLOW SPRINKLES

M&M'S

RED AND RAINBOW
SOUR STRAPS

SMARTIES

SNAKES

WAFFLE CONES

MENTOS

WAFFLE BASKET

BUTTERFLY SPRINKLES

RED LIQUORICE TUBES

NERDS

MACAROONS

RED AND BLUE SOUR TUBES

MILK CHOCOLATE MELTS

HONEYCOMB BAR

FLAKE BAR

CRUNCHIE BAR

WHITE CHOCOLATE MELTS

MONSTER 5'S GREEN SPRINKLES

JELLY BEANS

STRAWBERRIES & CREAM

TIC TACS

MILK CHOCOLATE FINGER BISCUITS

JUBES

LICORICE STRAP

LOLLIES

SPEARMINT LEAVES

JUBES

RASPBERRIES

LICORICE ALLSORTS

PINK AND WHITE LONG SPRINKLES

CHOCOLATE LADY BEETLES

MARSHMALLOW SWIRLS

MINI DROPS

MOIST COCONUT FLAKES

ROLL UP

DOMED MARSHMALLOWS

ARTS & PLAYTIME

artist's sketchbook

TAKES OVER 1 HOUR

Make this recipe a day ahead so that the ready-made icing dries hard enough to draw on.

EQUIPMENT

30cm (12-inch) square cake board

CAKE

20cm (8 inch) square cake

1 x 453g (14½-ounce) tub vanilla frosting

2 x 500g (1-pound) packets ready-made white icing

pure icing (confectioners') sugar, for dusting

DECORATIONS

non-toxic edible coloured markers

1 Level cake top. Secure cake, cut-side down, on cake board with a little frosting. Spread frosting over top and sides of cake.

2 Knead ready-made icing on a surface dusted with a little sifted icing sugar until icing loses its stickiness. Roll icing on a surface dusted with a little sifted icing sugar until large enough to cover cake (see page 114).

3 Using a rolling pin, lift the icing onto the cake. Dust your hands lightly with icing sugar; smooth icing over the cake. Trim icing neatly around base of cake; stand overnight to allow icing to firm.

4 Using coloured markers, let the kids go crazy and draw all over the cake themselves, or decorate with their favourite character.

test kitchen tips

If you prefer, you can buy food decorating pens online or at good cake decorating stores. If using butter cream instead of the vanilla frosting, you will need one quantity of butter cream (see page 110).

test kitchen tips

If you want a daytime scene,
colour the icing light blue and use
a yellow jube as the sun and the
sugar pearls to represent sun rays.
If using butter cream instead
of the vanilla frosting, you need
one quantity of butter cream
(see page 110).

cityscape at night

TAKES UP TO 1 HOUR

EQUIPMENT

25cm (10-inch) square cake board

small piping bag fitted with a small plain tube

CAKE

1 x 500g (1-pound) packaged chocolate block cake

1 x 453g (14½-ounce) tub vanilla frosting

dark blue food colouring

DECORATIONS

20cm (8-inch) strip licorice strap

4 lattice biscuits

13 yellow mini M&M's

½ teaspoon yellow soft sugar pearls

1 Secure cake to cake board with a little frosting.

2 Tint frosting dark blue with blue food colouring. Reserve 1 tablespoon of frosting; spread remaining over top and sides of cake.

3 Using picture as a guide, place licorice on cake to represent the road. Cut the biscuits into different lengths and widths to represent buildings; position on the cake above the road.

4 Spoon reserved frosting into the piping bag. Pipe a few dots of frosting in some of the 'windows' of the buildings and secure M&M's to biscuits for 'lights'.

5 Place pearls above the buildings for stars. Decorate with cars (see tip, below), if you like.

tip We used car patches available from craft and sewing stores. You could use small diecast cars from toy shops. Be aware of choking hazards if using small plastic cars.

tubby, the well-rounded bear

TAKES UP TO 30 MINUTES

EQUIPMENT

20cm (8-inch) round cake board

4 wooden toothpicks

1 small bamboo skewer

CAKE

5 cinnamon doughnuts

1 jam doughnut

2 mini doughnuts

1 tablespoon ready-made vanilla frosting

DECORATIONS

2 blue Smarties

1 brown Smartie

chocolate writing gel

40cm x 1cm (16-inch x ½-inch) wide ribbon

1 Secure one cinnamon doughnut to cake board with a little frosting, top with the jam doughnut, securing with a little frosting; top with another cinnamon doughnut, secure with a little frosting.

2 Cut one cinnamon doughnut in half crossways. Spread a little frosting on one cut-side of each half; attach to the body with a little frosting to form legs.

3 Cut one cinnamon doughnut in half crossways; secure to the bear using toothpicks to form arms.

4 Using picture as a guide, position remaining cinnamon doughnut, upright, on top to form the bear's head; secure with the bamboo skewer.

5 Cut one-third from each mini doughnut; reserve one larger offcut. Spread a little frosting over the cut sides of the smaller doughnuts; attach to head to form ears (secure with toothpicks if unstable). Trim one-third off the end of an offcut; use the rounded end to form the bear's nose, secure to the face with a little frosting.

6 Using a little frosting, attach the blue Smarties to the head for eyes, and the brown Smartie for a nose. Use chocolate writing gel to pipe mouth and pupils on bear. Use ribbon to make a bow; attach with a little icing, if you like (see tips, right).

test kitchen tips

For information on how to make a
bow, see page 115. Make sure that you
have removed all the toothpicks and
skewers before serving the bear.

test kitchen tips

Use hundreds and thousands as an alternative to the orange sprinkles. You can use cream-filled rollettes, if you prefer. If using butter cream instead of the vanilla frosting, you will need two quantities of butter cream (see page 110).

super-jumper's skipping rope

TAKES OVER 1 HOUR

EQUIPMENT

30cm x 40cm (12-inch x 16-inch) rectangular cake board

CAKE

1 x 450g (14½-ounce) packaged double unfilled sponge slabs

1 x 453g (14½-ounce) tub vanilla frosting

green and yellow food colouring

pure icing (confectioners') sugar, for dusting

DECORATIONS

3 cups (225g) moist coconut flakes

500g (1-pound) packet ready-made white icing

½ cup orange sprinkles

2 jam rollettes

1 Secure cakes, long sides together, on the cake board with a little frosting.

2 Reserve ½ cup of the frosting; tint remaining frosting green. Spread green frosting over top and sides of cake.

3 Tint coconut green (see page 112); press over the top and sides of cake.

4 Divide ready-made icing in half. Knead half the icing on a surface dusted with a little sifted icing sugar until icing loses its stickiness. Tint remaining icing yellow; knead on a surface dusted with a little sifted icing sugar until icing loses its stickiness. Roll yellow icing into a rope shape about 60cm x 5mm (24-inch x ¼-inch) thick. Repeat with white icing. Twist both icings together; gently roll to secure together. Cut a little round from each end of the rope, flatten slightly; reserve.

5 Place sprinkles in a shallow bowl. Spread the remaining frosting all over both rollettes; roll in sprinkles to coat.

6 Using picture as a guide, position rollettes on the cake to form skipping rope handles. Position rope on cake, gently pushing into the end of each rollette; attach the flattened icings on the other side of the rollettes to form rope knots.

ball sports

TAKES OVER 1 HOUR **MAKES** 12

The decorations will make 3 of each type of ball pictured here.

EQUIPMENT

5cm (2-inch) round cutter

20cm (8-inch) round or square cake board

CAKE

2 x 500g (1-pound) packaged chocolate block cakes

½ x 453g (14½-ounce) tub vanilla frosting

DECORATIONS

32 orange mini M&M's

56 red mini M&M's

50 yellow mini M&M's

50 green mini M&M's

42 white Tic Tacs

25cm (10-inch) licorice strap, sliced thinly

1 Using cutter, cut six rounds from each cake. Spread frosting over tops of cake rounds.
2 Using picture as a guide, decorate cakes with M&M's, Tic Tacs and licorice to form ball patterns. Secure cakes to board with a little frosting.

test kitchen tips

Turn these into garden beds by using M&M's to decorate the cakes as flowers for budding gardeners. Use a marble or butter cake, if you prefer. Double or triple the recipe to make more sport balls.

test kitchen tips

If using butter cream instead of ready-made frosting, you will need two quantities of butter cream (see page 110). We made the cupcakes here, instead of buying them, so we could tint the mixture in camouflage colours. To save time, decorate the tops of store-bought cupcakes with the camouflage icing.

camo cupcakes

TAKES OVER 1 HOUR (+ COOLING) **MAKES** 12

EQUIPMENT

12-hole (⅓-cup/80ml) standard muffin pan

12 dark green paper cupcake cases

4 paper piping bags (see page 113)

plastic wrap

CAKE

1 x 340g (11-ounce) packet golden butter cake

¼ cup (25g) cocoa powder

golden yellow, juniper green and moss green food colouring

1 x 453g (14½-ounce) tub vanilla frosting

cooking-oil spray

1 Preheat oven to 180°C/350°F. Line muffin pan with paper cases.

2 Make cake according to directions on packet. Divide mixture evenly among four small bowls: tint one bowl dark brown using 3 teaspoons sifted cocoa; tint one bowl light brown using 1 teaspoon sifted cocoa and yellow colouring; tint one bowl dark green using 2 teaspoons sifted cocoa and moss green colouring; and tint the remaining bowl a lighter green using juniper green colouring.

3 Drop teaspoons of alternate-coloured mixtures into paper cases – you need to drop 10 teaspoons of mixture into each paper case. Smooth surface; bake for 15 minutes. Stand cakes in pan for 5 minutes before turning, top-side up, onto a wire rack to cool.

4 Divide frosting evenly among four small bowls: tint one bowl dark brown using 3 teaspoons sifted cocoa, tint one bowl light brown using yellow colouring and 1 teaspoon sifted cocoa; tint one bowl dark green using 2 teaspoons sifted cocoa and moss green colouring; and tint the remaining bowl a lighter green using juniper green colouring.

5 Place each colour frosting into a paper piping bag; snip ends to make a 5mm (¼-inch) opening. Using picture as a guide, pipe frosting, in random spots, over cupcakes to create a camouflage pattern.

6 Lightly spray cooking-oil over a small piece of plastic wrap. Place plastic wrap, oiled-side down, over a cupcake and press lightly to flatten frosting. Remove plastic; repeat with remaining cupcakes.

lamington checkers

TAKES UP TO 30 MINUTES

EQUIPMENT

40cm (16-inch) square cake board

CAKE

3 x 360g (11½-ounce) packets lamingtons

DECORATIONS

18 mini chocolate cream-filled biscuits

½ x 453g (14½-ounce) tub vanilla frosting

1 Cut 18 lamingtons in half widthways. Using picture as guide, position the lamingtons in a checkerboard pattern on the cake board.
2 Spread the tops of half the biscuits with frosting. Using picture as a guide, position biscuits on the checkerboard.

test kitchen tip

Pink lamingtons, available
from supermarkets, would
make a pretty checkerboard
cake for a little girl's party.

test kitchen tips

Use Skittles as an alternative to the mini M&M's. Store the cakes in an airtight container in a cool dark place. Refrigerating the cakes will cause the colour on the M&M's to run. If using butter cream instead of the vanilla frosting, you will need one quantity of butter cream (see page 110).

gumball machines

TAKES OVER 1 HOUR (+ REFRIGERATION) **MAKES** 6

EQUIPMENT

35cm (14-inch) square cake board

oven tray

plastic wrap

CAKE

1 x 450g (14½-ounce) packaged double unfilled sponge slabs

1 x 453g (14½-ounce) tub vanilla frosting

red food colouring

6 mini double chocolate muffins

DECORATIONS

1 x 160g (5-ounce) packet mini M&M's

red writing icing

6 white chocolate Melts

1 Blend or process sponge cakes into crumbs. Combine cake crumbs and ⅓ cup of frosting in a large bowl. Roll ½ cups of mixture into six balls. Place on an oven tray; loosely cover with plastic wrap. Refrigerate for 2 hours or until firm.

2 Divide remaining frosting into two bowls. Tint one bowl with red colouring. Remove paper cases from muffins; trim tops from muffins so they are flat. Spread base and sides of muffins with red frosting. Secure muffins, cut-side down, on the cake board with a little frosting.

3 Place M&M's in a shallow bowl. Spread white frosting all over cake balls; roll cake balls evenly in M&M's to cover. Secure balls on top of muffins.

4 Use writing icing to pipe numbers on chocolate buttons (the number can be the birthday child's age). Secure buttons on muffins.

a frosty winter's castle

TAKES OVER 1 HOUR

You need 3 round cakes for this recipe.

EQUIPMENT

35cm (14-inch) round cake board

8cm (3¾-inch) round cutter

3 long bamboo skewers

CAKE

1½ x 460g (14½-ounce) packaged double unfilled sponge cake rounds

2 x 453g (14½-ounce) tubs vanilla frosting

1 x 250g (8-ounce) packet jam rollettes

DECORATIONS

3 mini waffle ice-cream cones

1 cup (80g) desiccated coconut

3 flag cake toppers

2 ice-cream wafers

8 x 250g (8-ounce) packets marshmallows (use white marshmallows only)

1 Secure one round cake to the cake board with a little frosting. Reserve ¼ cup of frosting. Sandwich second cake on top of the cake on the board with a little frosting. Spread top and sides with half the remaining frosting.

2 Place the 8cm cutter on top of the remaining cake; using the cutter as a guide, cut an 8cm round from the cake. Place the cake round in the centre of the iced cake; spread top and sides with frosting.

3 Thread three jam rollettes onto a bamboo skewer. Repeat with remaining rollettes to make three towers. Spread top and sides with remaining frosting. Arrange towers around the base of the cake.

4 Place reserved frosting in a microwave-safe bowl. Heat frosting in microwave oven on MEDIUM (50%) for 10 seconds or until slightly melted; drizzle over top of cones. Sprinkle with coconut. Gently push cake topper into top of each cone. Position cones on top of each tower.

5 Cut wafers into door and window shapes. Using picture as a guide, decorate cake with marshmallows. Position wafer door and windows, securing with a little frosting as necessary.

tip We only used the white marshmallows from the packets of marshmallows; serve the pink marshmallows at the party. You can make the castle pink and white if you like; in this case you will only need 4 packets of marshmallows.

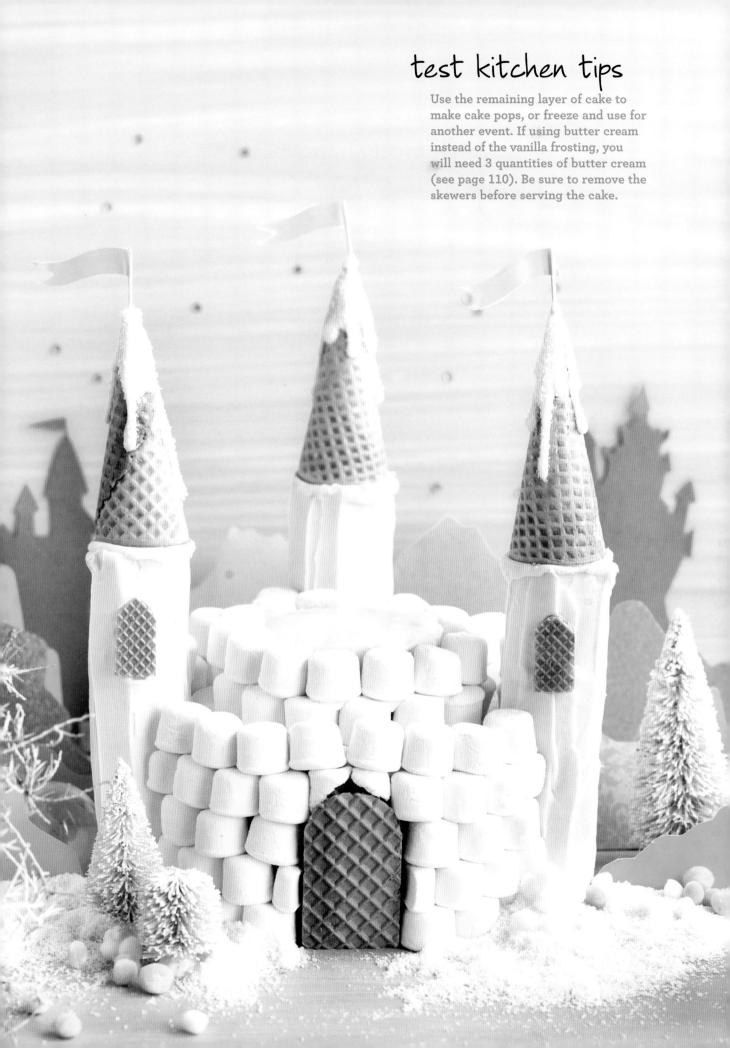

test kitchen tips

Use the remaining layer of cake to make cake pops, or freeze and use for another event. If using butter cream instead of the vanilla frosting, you will need 3 quantities of butter cream (see page 110). Be sure to remove the skewers before serving the cake.

ice-cream sundaes

TAKES UP TO 1 HOUR (+ REFRIGERATION) **MAKES** 8

EQUIPMENT

20cm (8-inch) round or square cake board

oven tray

plastic wrap

CAKE

8 cups (900g) cake crumbs (see tips)

2 x 453g (14½-ounce) tubs vanilla frosting

8 ice-cream waffle baskets

½ cup (170g) tub chocolate frosting

DECORATIONS

2 tablespoons hundreds and thousands

8 red glacé cherries

1 Place cake crumbs in a large bowl. Add ½ cup vanilla frosting; stir to combine. Roll ⅔-cups of mixture into eight balls. Place on an oven tray; loosely cover with plastic wrap. Refrigerate for 2 hours or until firm.

2 Place remaining vanilla frosting in a microwave-safe jug. Microwave frosting on HIGH (100%) for 10 seconds or until melted slightly. Carefully pour frosting over balls; stand until frosting sets slightly. Place balls in wafer baskets. Secure baskets to cake board with a little frosting.

3 Place chocolate frosting in a microwave-safe jug. Microwave on HIGH (100%) for 10 seconds or until melted slightly. Carefully pour chocolate over balls; scatter with hundreds and thousands, then top with cherries.

test kitchen tips

We used one double unfilled sponge to make 4 cups of cake crumbs. This recipe is easy to double or triple. If using butter cream instead of the vanilla frosting, you will need one quantity of butter cream (see page 110).

wrapped up like a mummy

TAKES UP TO 1 HOUR **MAKES** 12

These cute little cakes would also be a welcome treat at a halloween party for younger children.

EQUIPMENT

35cm (14-inch) square cake board

CAKE

12 x un-iced standard cupcakes

1 x 453g (14½-ounce) tub vanilla frosting

DECORATIONS

400g (12½-ounce) packet Minties

24 red mini M&M's

1 Spread frosting over top of cupcakes.

2 Unwrap Minties. Place one Mintie at a time on a small microwave-safe plate; heat in the microwave on MEDIUM-HIGH (75%) for 5 seconds or until Mintie has softened. (Be careful as Minties may be very hot.)

3 When cool enough to handle, carefully stretch the Mintie, pulling it into thin strips. Cut the strips into lengths long enough to fit across the top of the cupcake. Lay strips of stretched Minties over cupcakes, overlapping to represent a mummy's bandage. Repeat with the remaining cupcakes and Minties.

4 Position M&Ms on cakes for eyes.

test kitchen tips

Cupcakes should be decorated the day of serving as the Minties will dissolve if left overnight. Store cakes in an airtight container at room temperature. If using butter cream instead of vanilla frosting, you need half a quantity of butter cream (see page 110). If you can't find un-iced cupcakes, use iced ones and trim the icing from the cakes.

test kitchen tips

If using butter cream instead of vanilla frosting, you will need half a quantity of butter cream (see page 110). We used a selection of small jelly beans, rainbow choc chips and M&M's for the treasure.

pirate's treasure

TAKES UP TO 1 HOUR **MAKES** 12

You will need 3 x 4-pack (460g) double chocolate chip muffins for this cake.

EQUIPMENT

40cm (16-inch) square cake board

CAKE

12 double chocolate chip muffins

1 x 453g (14½-ounce) tub vanilla frosting

green food colouring

DECORATIONS

1½ cups small mixed lollies

1 x 50g (1½-ounce) chocolate-coated honeycomb bar, or plain honeycomb

assorted pirate toys

red decorating icing

1 Using a small sharp knife, cut the peak off the top of each muffin; reserve. Dig about 1 tablespoon out of each muffin centre and discard.

2 Divide mixed lollies evenly into the centres of each muffin. Top with 2 tablespoons of frosting, top with reserved muffin pieces.

3 Tint remaining frosting green. Spread muffins with frosting.

4 Discard chocolate from honeycomb if necessary; break honeycomb into pieces. Using picture as a guide, decorate cakes with honeycomb and assorted pirate toys. On one cake draw an 'X' with the red decorating icing using a flat piping nozzle (these come with the icing tube). Position cakes on cake board; secure with a little frosting.

I can see a rainbow

TAKES OVER 1 HOUR (+ COOLING) **MAKES** 12

EQUIPMENT

12-hole (⅓-cup/80ml) standard muffin pan

12 coloured paper cases

6 small ziptop plastic bags

CAKE

1 x 340g (11-ounce) packet butter cake mix

red, yellow, green, orange, purple and blue food colouring

1 x 453g (14½-ounce) tub vanilla frosting

DECORATIONS

red, yellow, green, orange, purple and blue sprinkles

1 Preheat oven to 160°C/325°F. Line muffin pan with paper cases.

2 Make cake according to instructions on packet. Divide mixture evenly between 6 bowls and tint red, yellow, green, orange, purple and blue. Spoon each colour into a separate ziptop bag; snip off the corner. Pipe the red cake mixture into the centre of each paper case. Push the corner of the yellow ziptop bag into the centre of the red cake mix and pipe in the yellow cake mixture. Repeat with remaining green, orange, purple and blue mixtures. Bake for 15 minutes; stand cakes in pan for 5 minutes before turning, top-side up, onto a wire rack to cool.

3 Divide frosting into 6 small bowls; tint red, yellow, green, orange, purple and blue. Spread a different colour frosting over two of the cupcakes; then using the picture as a guide, decorate the cupcakes with matching sprinkles.

4 Position cupcakes on the cake board; secure with a little frosting.

test kitchen tips

If using butter cream instead of the vanilla frosting you will need one quantity of butter cream (see page 110). We used paper cases to match each colour of the cupcakes. We made the cupcakes instead of buying them, so we could tint the mixture in rainbow colours. To save time, decorate the tops of store-bought cupcakes with the different-coloured icings.

test kitchen tip

If using butter cream instead of the vanilla frosting, you will need one quantity of butter cream (see page 110). Colour 2 cups of desiccated coconut with yellow food colouring (see page 112) to decorate the cake board.

grommet's surfboard

TAKES UP TO 1 HOUR

EQUIPMENT

30cm x 40cm (12-inch x 16-inch) rectangular cake board

CAKE

1 x 450g (14½-ounce) packaged double unfilled sponge slabs

1 x 453g (14½-ounce) tub vanilla frosting

DECORATIONS

20g (¾ ounce) dark chocolate Melts

1 red sour bootlace

2 yellow sour bootlaces

3 rainbow sour straps

120cm (8-inch) licorice strap, trimmed to 3mm (⅛-inch) thick

2 white milk bottles

1 yellow milk bottle

1 Position cakes on the cake board so short ends of sponge are together.

2 Using a small serrated knife, trim sides of cake to form a surfboard shape. Discard trimmed pieces. Secure cake to cake board with a little frosting.

3 Spread frosting over top and sides of cake.

4 Melt chocolate (see page 115). Cool slightly.

5 Using picture as a guide, position bootlaces down the centre of the board, trim to fit. Brush sour straps with a little water to remove sugar; position across surfboard on a slight angle, trim to fit. Position licorice strap at the end of the cake to create a leg rope on the surfboard, secure with a little melted chocolate.

6 Cut each white milk bottle lengthways into three pieces; position five pieces on the rainbow strap to form a flower shape; cut the top from the yellow milk bottle; secure to the middle of the flower with a little melted chocolate.

drum roll, please

TAKES OVER 1 HOUR

EQUIPMENT

1 x 20cm (8-inch) cardboard cake board

2 x 8cm (3¼-inch) cardboard cake boards

paper piping bag (see page 113)

50cm (20-inch) square cake board

CAKE

1 x 460g (14½-ounce) packaged double unfilled sponge cake rounds

1 quantity white chocolate ganache (see page 110)

1 x 453g (14½-ounce) tub vanilla frosting

6 packaged pavlova nests (80g)

DECORATIONS

6 x 25g (¾-ounce) packets orange sprinkles

375g (12 ounces) white chocolate Melts

100g (3 ounces) white chocolate Melts, extra

2 chocolate cream wafer sticks

2 blue sprinkle licorice allsorts

14 chocolate wafer sticks

16 blue Smarties

1 Level cake tops. Secure one cake onto the 20cm cake board with a little ganache. Spread the top of the cake with ½ cup ganache; top with remaining cake, cut-side down. Spread sides of the cake with frosting. Place sprinkles in a baking tray; roll cake on its side to cover in sprinkles (see page 113).

2 Secure two pavlovas to the 8cm cake boards with a little ganache; spread tops with ¼ cup ganache. Top each with another pavlova; spread tops with ¼ cup ganache then top with remaining pavlovas. Spread sides of pavlovas with frosting; carefully roll in sprinkles.

3 Draw a 20cm (8-inch) and two 8cm (3¼-inch) circles on baking paper.

4 Melt chocolate (see page 115); spread into each baking-paper circle to form three discs. Stand for 10 minutes or until set. Remove baking paper, and secure chocolate discs to the top of the cake and pavlovas with a little frosting.

5 Melt extra chocolate. Fill paper piping bag with chocolate, snip a small opening in the end; pipe a little chocolate onto one end of each cream wafer stick; attach licorice allsort to make drumsticks, stand until set.

6 Assemble drum kit on the 50cm cake board as pictured, secure with a little ganache. Using picture as a guide, decorate sides of large drum cake with wafer sticks and blue Smarties, securing with a little melted chocolate. Secure drumsticks to cake with a little melted chocolate.

test kitchen tips

We used ganache in this recipe to hold the larger drum in place as it sets firmer than the frosting. If using butter cream instead of the vanilla frosting, you will need one quantity of butter cream (see page 110).

test kitchen tips

If using butter cream instead of the vanilla frosting, you will need one quantity of butter cream (see page 110). Look for cakes with slightly domed tops, otherwise you will have to trim the cake tops to create the curved book shape.

oops, I did it again!

TAKES OVER 1 HOUR

You will need two slab cakes for this recipe.

EQUIPMENT

30cm x 40cm (12-inch x16-inch) rectangular cake board

wooden skewer

CAKE

1 x 450g (14½-ounce) packaged double unfilled sponge slabs

1 x 453g (14½-ounce) tub vanilla frosting

DECORATIONS

blue, red, green writing icing

3 blueberry licorice tubes

1 raspberry licorice tube

blue and red decorating icing

40cm (16-inch) black licorice strap, cut into a thin strip

6 red sour straps

1 Secure cakes, long sides together, on the cake board with a little frosting. Shape cake if necessary into a book shape (see tips). Spread frosting over top and sides of cake.

2 Draw lines on cake with blue writing icing.

3 Cut blueberry and raspberry licorice tubes into desired length for pens; trim one end into a point using a small sharp knife. Pipe a little blue and red decorating icing on the points of each lolly for pen nibs.

4 Place black licorice strip down the middle of the cakes. Decorate base of cake with sour straps trimming to fit around cake. Outline the top of the sour strap with red writing icing.

5 Using green and red writing icing, and picture as a guide, decorate cake; you could make it a maths book, as we have done here, or write a poem, a short story or draw pictures on the book.

SCIENCE & NATURE

balloon with a view

TAKES UP TO **1 HOUR**

EQUIPMENT

30cm x 40cm (12-inch x16-inch) rectangular cake board

CAKE

1 x 460g (14½-ounce) packaged double unfilled sponge cake rounds

1 x 453g (14½-ounce) tub strawberry frosting

DECORATIONS

2 x 175g (5½ ounce) packet berry delight marshmallow swirls

¼ cup (35g) white chocolate Melts

1 waffle basket (15g)

3 rainbow sour straps, yellow part only, trimmed into 3mm (⅛-inch) thick strips

1 Secure one cake to the cake board with a little frosting. Spread cake top with a little frosting; top with remaining cake. Using a small serrated knife; trim top edge of cake to create a dome shape. Spread frosting all over top and sides of cake.

2 Using picture as a guide, position marshmallows in coloured lines over cake.

3 Melt chocolate (see page 115); cool slightly. Cut waffle basket in half crossways with a bread knife. Secure basket on its side, with a little melted chocolate, onto the cake board.

4 Attach sour strap to basket with a little melted chocolate, push other end of strap into balloon.

test kitchen tips

You can also use raspberry and vanilla marshmallows, halved crossways, or a variety of chocolate buttons to decorate the balloon. If using butter cream instead of the strawberry frosting, you will need one quantity of butter cream – you can tint it pink or leave it plain (see page 110).

test kitchen tips

Other sweets, such as flake or chocolate-coated honeycomb, can be crushed and used as gravel on the road. If using butter cream instead of the chocolate frosting, you will need two quantities of chocolate butter cream (see page 110). Remember to remove all non-edible toys before serving.

CONSTRUCTION ZONE CONSTRUCTION ZONE

heavy lifter road crew

TAKES UP TO 30 MINUTES

You will need four slab cakes for this recipe.

EQUIPMENT

30cm x 40cm (12-inch x16-inch) rectangular cake board

CAKE

2 x 450g (14½-ounce) packaged double unfilled sponge slabs

1 x 453g (14½-ounce) tub dark chocolate frosting

DECORATION

1 x 30g (1-ounce) chocolate flake

1 x 40g (1½-ounce) chocolate-coated honeycomb bar, or plain honeycomb

24 brown chocolate drops

20 brown mini M&M's

¼ cup chocolate sprinkles

½ teaspoon yellow nerds

small toy digger trucks and construction toys

1 Secure two cakes, side-by-side, on the cake board with a little frosting. Spread frosting over top of the cake. Cut remaining cakes into large pieces and stack on top of cake on cake board, securing with a little frosting. Using a small sharp knife; trim cake to form a mound.

2 Using a small serrated knife; cut into cake to create a 5cm (2-inch) wide sloping roadway around the cake, leading to the top of the cake.

3 Spread cake all over with remaining frosting. Cut flake into three pieces. Trim and discard chocolate from honeycomb bar if necessary; roughly chop honeycomb into small chunks.

4 Using picture as a guide, decorate cake with flakes, honeycomb, chocolate drops, M&M's, sprinkles and nerds. Position toys on cake.

around the old campfire

TAKES OVER 1 HOUR

EQUIPMENT

30cm (12-inch) round cake board

plastic sandwich bag

oven trays

CAKE

2 x 600g (1¼-pound) packaged round chocolate mud cakes

1½ x 453g (14½-ounce) tubs dark chocolate frosting

DECORATIONS

5 orange lollypops

5 yellow lollypops

5 red lollypops

4 x 30g (1-ounce) chocolate flakes

2 x 125g (4-ounce) packets chocolate finger biscuits

1 Preheat oven to 150°C/300°F. Line a baking tray with baking paper.

2 Split each cake in half. Secure one cake round to the cake board with a little frosting; spread ⅓ cup frosting over cake, top with another cake round. Repeat with ⅓ cup icing and one more cake round. (Reserve the remaining cake round for another use – you could use it to make cake pops). Spread the remaining frosting over sides and top of cake.

3 Place lollypops in the plastic bag; using a rolling pin or meat mallet, gently smash the lollypops until broken into pieces; discard sticks. Place lollypop pieces onto the baking tray; place in oven for 5 minutes or until melted and the edges are starting to brown. Cool on tray; set aside until needed.

4 Carefully cut flakes in half crossways. Break melted lollypops into large shards. Using picture as a guide, arrange toffee shards on cake to form the fire; arrange flakes around toffee for logs. Position chocolate fingers around side of the cake.

test kitchen tips

If using butter cream instead of the chocolate frosting, you will need two quantities of chocolate butter cream (see page 110). Use a variety of chocolate bars – such as Flakes, Violet Crumbles or Tim Tam biscuits – for the campfire logs. The melted lollipops are best made on day of serving as humidity may cause them to dissolve.

test kitchen tips

We've use a mixture of lollies to turn this into a rubbish bin. To make this a recycle bin, use a variety of milk bottles. Save any licorice off-cuts for another use.

doing the right thing

TAKES OVER 1 HOUR

EQUIPMENT

20cm (8-inch) square cake board

CAKE

2 x 450g (14½-ounce) packaged double unfilled sponge slabs

2 quantities butter cream (see page 110)

red food colouring

DECORATIONS

3 white milk bottle lollies

4 cola bottles

4 blue sprinkle licorice allsorts

10 assorted coloured M&M's

4 snake lollies

2 red licorice tubes

½ x 240g (7½-ounce) packet black licorice strap

2 red M&M's

1 Sandwich three sponges together upright with a little butter cream. Use a serrated knife to trim two long sides of cake into a wheelie bin shape (make the top edge into a 12cm (4¾-inch) square and the bottom edge 11cm (4½-inch) square.

2 Secure cake onto the cake board with a little butter cream. Tint remaining butter cream red; spread three-quarters of the butter cream over the top and sides of cake.

3 Position lollies over top of cake.

4 Use a serrated knife to trim remaining sponge into a 12cm (4¾-inch) square. Split cake in half; spread remaining butter cream all over top, sides and base of one cake. (Discard or reserve the remaining cake piece for another use).

5 Place the cake at an angle over the top of the lollies to create a lid; secure licorice tubes to the top to form handles.

6 Unroll each licorice strap until you are left with a 4cm (1½-inch) round; trim away unrolled pieces. Cut licorice rounds in half through the centre to make two wheels. Position wheels on the cake; secure M&M's to the centre of the wheels with a little butter cream.

butterfly display case

TAKES OVER 1 HOUR

You need one slab cake for this recipe.

EQUIPMENT

30cm (12-inch) square cake board

paper piping bag (see page 113)

CAKE

½ x 450g (14½-ounce) packaged double unfilled sponge slabs

½ cup (170g) tub cream cheese frosting

½ cup (170g) tub dark chocolate frosting

DECORATIONS

⅓ cup (50g) milk chocolate Melts

5 x 30g (1-ounce) chocolate Flakes

8 chocolate finger biscuits

1 rainbow berry roll-up

1 rainbow roll-up

2 red licorice tubes

1 Level cake top. Secure cake, cut-side down, on the cake board with a little cream cheese frosting. Spread chocolate frosting over sides of cake. Spread cream cheese frosting over top of cake.

2 Melt chocolate (see page 115). Using picture as a guide, cut and position Flakes for the frame. Place the melted chocolate into a piping bag; snip end to make a small opening. Pipe chocolate onto the corners of the frame to secure the Flakes together. Secure biscuits on each corner of the frame with a little melted chocolate.

3 Using a pair of sharp scissors, cut butterfly shapes from roll-ups. Trim excess to make antennae and wing decorations.

4 Using picture as a guide, secure butterflies to cake with a little melted chocolate; attach licorice in the middle of the wings for bodies, then attach antennae and wing decorations.

test kitchen tips

Freeze the remaining cake for another use, or crumble and make cake pops decorated to match your party theme. If using butter cream instead of the cream cheese frosting, you will need to make one quantity of butter cream (see page 110). Tint half the mixture light yellow; add 1½ tablespoons cocoa to the remaining mixture for chocolate butter cream.

test kitchen tips

Use any lollies you like, but make sure they match the colours of the barrels. Cones can be painted a day ahead; store in an airtight container. Don't refrigerate as the cones will go soft and the lolly colours may bleed. The cake can be made a day ahead; store in a cool dark place. If using butter cream instead of the frosting, you will need one quantity of chocolate butter cream (see page 110).

science experiment spill

TAKES OVER 1 HOUR

EQUIPMENT

30cm (12-inch) round cake board

small new artists' paint brush

CAKE

2 x 20cm (8-inch) round chocolate cakes

1 x 453g (14½-ounce) tub dark chocolate frosting

½ x 453g (14½-ounce) tub vanilla frosting

orange, red, yellow and green food colouring

DECORATIONS

½ x 80g (2½-ounce) packet wafer biscuits

4 flat-bottomed ice-cream cones

1 teaspoon each green and yellow nerds

1 teaspoon red rainbow choc chips

65cm (26-inch) tape or ribbon (see tip this page)

1 Level cake tops. Secure one cake, cut-side down, on the cake board. Spread cake top with ⅓ cup of chocolate frosting; top with remaining cake. Spread chocolate frosting over top and side of cake.

2 Brush wafers with orange colouring mixed with a little water to make wire fence. Position wafers around side of cake. Wrap tape around cake, secure with a little frosting, if needed.

3 Trim the tops of the ice-cream cones from the bases with a serrated knife. Paint two tops with the yellow colouring mixed with a little water; stand for 10 minutes or until dry. Paint two tops with the green colouring mixed with a little water; stand for 10 minutes or until dry. Paint two bases with red colouring mixed with a little water; stand for 10 minutes or until dry. Discard the remaining two ice-cream bases. Stack the ice-cream cones, top ends together, to form barrels; secure with a little frosting.

4 Divide vanilla frosting between three microwave safe bowls. Tint red, yellow and green. Heat frostings in a microwave oven on MEDIUM (50%) for about 20 seconds or until melted.

5 Using picture as a guide, position barrels on cake; fill barrels with frosting; decorate with nerds and red choc chips. Pour remaining warmed frosting on top of cake, allowing it to spill over the sides.

tip The biohazard tape was ordered online from the US. Printing the words 'biohazard' onto yellow tape with a permanent marker adds a visual effect which is just as good, and less expensive.

robbie 2.0

TAKES OVER 1 HOUR

EQUIPMENT

30cm x 40cm (12-inch x 16-inch) rectangular cake board

2 bamboo skewers

CAKE

2 x 450g (14½-ounce) packaged double unfilled sponge slabs

2 quantities butter cream (see page 110)

blue and red food colouring

DECORATIONS

12 vanilla macaroons (see tip)

2 blue sour tubes, halved

6 blue licorice allsorts

5 each of yellow and red fruit rolls

1 red licorice tube

3 x 1m (1 yard) black licorice strap

6 licorice allsorts, blue part only

6 heart-shaped jubes

4 green fruit rolls

4 white chocolate Melts

⅓ x 180g block white chocolate

1 each of blue, red, yellow and green M&M's

4 each of yellow, orange and red mini M&M's

1 Secure two sponges onto the cake board with a little butter cream. Using a serrated knife, cut one of the remaining sponges into a 12cm (4¾-inch) square. Cut the remaining cake into a 14cm x 4cm (5½-inch x 1½-inch) rectangle. Using picture as a guide, secure cakes to the cake board with a little butter cream.

2 Tint two-thirds of the butter cream blue. Tint remaining butter cream red.

3 Using picture as a guide, spread the blue butter cream over the top and sides of robot body. Spread the red butter cream over top and sides of head. Position macaroons as robots arms; secure with a little butter cream.

4 Push two of the sour tube halves onto skewers; place a blue allsort on one end and a red and yellow fruit roll on the other end. Push into cake as antennae. Secure remaining sour tubes to make the mouth.

5 Cut two red fruit rolls into claws, as pictured; secure to the end of the macaroons.

6 Trim the red licorice tube into an arrow shape. Using picture as a guide, decorate robot's head and body with the remaining lollies; secure decorations with a little butter cream.

tip Macaroons are available from speciality bakery shops and select supermarkets. If you can't find them, any small round filled biscuit will do. Try mini Oreos or Wagon Wheels, or Monte Carlos.

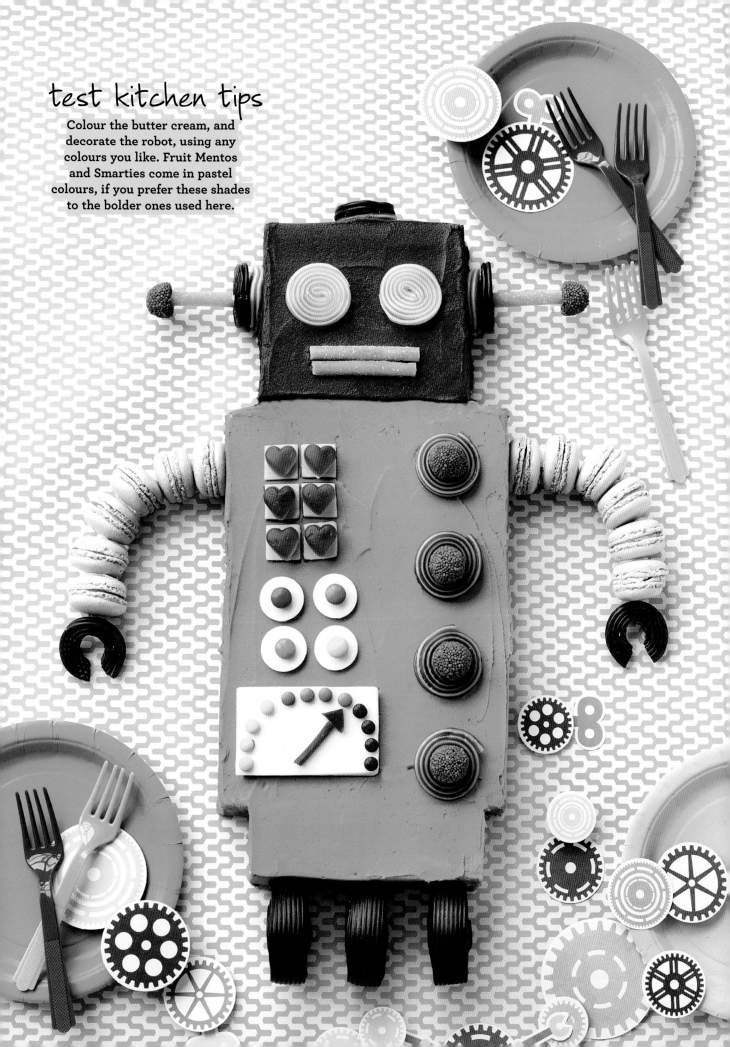

test kitchen tips

Colour the butter cream, and decorate the robot, using any colours you like. Fruit Mentos and Smarties come in pastel colours, if you prefer these shades to the bolder ones used here.

big rig petrol tanker

TAKES OVER 1 HOUR

EQUIPMENT

30cm x 40cm (12-inch x 16-inch) rectangular cake board

CAKE

11 banana-flavoured muffin bars (460g)

2 x 500g (1-pound) honey sponge rolls

2 x 453g (14½-ounce) tubs vanilla frosting

yellow and black food colouring

DECORATIONS

3½ x 240g (7½-ounce) packets black licorice straps

14 Milky Bar buttons

1 red sour strap

5 red sour bootlaces

5 red sour tubes

4 orange mini M&M's

2 yellow mini chocolate drops

6 yellow mini M&M's

1 Secure 8 muffins, side-by-side in a single line, on the cake board with a little frosting. Secure sponge rolls on top of the muffins with a little frosting.

2 Reserve ½ cup of the frosting. Tint remaining frosting yellow. Spread yellow frosting all over sponge rolls and muffins.

3 Position remaining muffins at the front end of the trailer to create the driver's cab; secure with a little frosting. Tint reserved frosting grey with black colouring. Spread grey frosting all over sides and top of cab.

4 Unroll each licorice strap until you are left with a 6cm (2½-inch) diameter roll; trim away unrolled pieces. Cut licorice rolls in half to make 'wheels'. Position wheels on cake (you need 14 wheels). Secure milky bar buttons to wheels with a little frosting. Trim remaining licorice to make two mud guards and windows; position on cab.

5 Cut two small stars from sour strap; position on cake as pictured. Using picture as a guide, decorate tanker with bootlaces. Cut 3 sour tubes in half crossways, position on cake to form front grill. Trim bootlace to fit across front of cab and back of tanker. Position orange M&M's as headlights and brake lights. Using picture as a guide, decorate cab with yellow chocolate drops and mini M&M's for rig lights. Attach remaining sour tubes as exhaust pipes.

volcano vomitus

TAKES OVER 1 HOUR

EQUIPMENT

oven tray

30cm (12-inch) round cake board

sandwich bag

CAKE

1 x 460g (14½-ounce) packaged double unfilled sponge cake rounds

1 cinnamon donut

1 x 453g (14½-ounce) tub dark chocolate frosting

1 x 453g (14½-ounce) tub vanilla frosting

yellow and orange food colouring

DECORATIONS

50g (1½ ounces) orange boiled lollies or barley sugar

50g (1½ ounces) red boiled lollies

50g (1½ ounces) yellow boiled lollies

1 cup (75g) moist coconut flakes

2 x 50g (1½ ounce) chocolate-coated honeycomb or plain honeycomb

¼ cup (65g) orange nerds (see tips)

1 Preheat oven to 150°C/300°F. Line an oven tray with baking paper.

2 Secure one cake to the cake board with a little frosting. Spread cake top with ⅓ cup of chocolate frosting; top with remaining cake. Using a small serrated knife, trim cake into a volcano shape. Secure donut to the top of the cake with a little frosting. Spread remaining chocolate frosting over top and sides of cake.

3 Place boiled lollies into the sandwich bag and gently smash with a rolling pin or meat mallet until broken into small pieces. Place pieces onto the oven tray; place in oven for 10 minutes or until lollies have melted. Use the back of a metal spoon to thin out edges. Cool toffee on tray.

4 Discard chocolate coating from honeycomb, if necessary. Roughly chop honeycomb.

5 Tint coconut yellow (see page 112). Using picture as a guide, position coconut, honeycomb and nerds around the base and sides of the volcano. Tint the vanilla frosting orange in a small microwave safe bowl. Heat frosting in a microwave oven on MEDIUM (50%) for 20 seconds or until melted.

6 Pour orange frosting around the top and down the sides of the volcano. Break cooled toffee into pieces; position in the top of the volcano as fire.

test kitchen tips

The toffee is best made on the day of serving. You could use red and yellow lollipops to make the toffee following step 3. If using butter cream instead of the frostings, you will need one quantity of chocolate butter cream and one quantity of plain butter cream (see page 110). You need to buy a packet of rainbow nerds, as these contain orange nerds.

test kitchen tips

Use any critter lollies you can find, sour worms work well, or even use plastic spiders, if you like. If using non-edible decorations, make sure they are removed before serving. If using butter cream instead of the vanilla frosting, you will need one quantity of butter cream (see page 110).

bug catcher

TAKES UP TO 1 HOUR

EQUIPMENT

20cm x 30cm (8-inch x 12-inch) rectangular
cake board

CAKE

1 x 450g (14½ ounce) packaged double unfilled
sponge slabs

1 x 453g (14½-ounce) tub vanilla frosting

DECORATIONS

¼ cup (45g) milk choc Bits

¼ cup (45g) dark choc Bits

26 spearmint leaves, halved

9 chocolate ladybirds

1 Position one cake lengthways on the cake board;
secure with a little frosting. Secure the remaining
cake, crossways, touching the top edge of the first
cake with a little frosting.

2 Using a small serrated knife, cut the upper cake
to create a funnel shape. Spread frosting over top
and sides of cakes.

3 Decorate the bottom edge of the cake with
combined choc Bits for 'dirt'. Using picture as a
guide, decorate the cake with spearmint leaves
and ladybirds.

tip We used Tic Tacs to make the ladybird 'trail'.
Use as many ladybirds as you like to decorate the
cake board.

a blizzard of snowmen

TAKES UP TO 30 MINUTES MAKES 6

EQUIPMENT

6 serving plates, or a large serving tray

CAKE

½ cup (80g) icing (confectioners') sugar

6 jam doughnuts

6 cinnamon doughnuts

6 mini cinnamon doughnuts

½ cup (170g) ready-made vanilla frosting

DECORATIONS

12 small clean sticks, or brown pipe cleaners

12 brown mini M&M's

6 orange jelly babies

1 Place sifted icing sugar on a large plate. Roll jam doughnuts in icing sugar to coat. Repeat with cinnamon doughnuts and mini doughnuts.

2 Secure jam doughnuts on serving plates with a little frosting. Top with cinnamon doughnuts and mini doughnuts to create snowmen, securing each doughnut with a little frosting.

3 Insert sticks into cinnamon doughnuts to form arms. Secure mini M&M's with a little frosting to form eyes. Trim jelly babies into wedges to create carrot noses. Insert into centre of mini doughnut.

test kitchen tip

Use a mixture of jam and cinnamon doughnuts, mini jam doughnuts and doughnut holes, if you like.

free-range chickens

TAKES UP TO 1 HOUR MAKES 6

CAKE

½ x 453g (14½-ounce) tub vanilla frosting

yellow food colouring

6 mini doughnuts

6 cinnamon doughnuts

DECORATIONS

1 cup (70g) moist coconut flakes

12 blue mini M&M's

6 mini white marshmallows, halved

black decorating gel

12 orange mini M&M's

1 Tint frosting with yellow colouring. Tint the coconut yellow (see page 112).

2 Spread frosting over mini doughnuts; roll in coconut to coat. Stand the doughnuts in the centre of the cinnamon doughnuts.

3 Position the blue M&M's on marshmallow halves with a little frosting; pipe black dots for pupils with decorating gel, secure on coconut for eyes. Position the orange M&M's to form beaks.

test kitchen tip
Use iced chocolate doughnuts as nests instead of the cinnamon doughnuts.

CREATURES

rainbow fish

TAKES UP TO 1 HOUR

EQUIPMENT

20 x 30cm (8-inch x12-inch) rectangular
cake board

CAKE

2 x 600g (1¼-pound) packaged white chocolate
mud cakes

1 x 453g (14½-ounce) tub vanilla frosting

blue food colouring

DECORATIONS

1 x 300g (9½-ounce) packet jubes

4 rainbow sour straps

1 white marshmallow, halved crossways

1 round black jube, halved crossways

1 white Tic Tac, halved crossways

2 red jelly beans

1 Secure one cake to the cake board with a little
frosting. Using picture as a guide, cut tail and fin
shapes from the second cake; secure to the cake
with a little frosting.
2 Tint frosting blue; spread over the top and sides
of cake.
3 Using oiled scissors, cut the jubes in half
crossways; using the picture as a guide, decorate
fish with jubes as scales. Trim the sour straps and use
to make a tail fin. Position the marshmallow, black
jube and tic tac on the cake for an eye; secure with
a little frosting. Position jelly beans for mouth.

test kitchen tips

You can use jelly beans or rainbow straps to decorate the fish. If using butter cream instead of the vanilla frosting, you will need one quantity of butter cream (see page 110).

test kitchen tips

Using natural almonds, which retain the brown skin, gives the owl's feathers a good definition, but you can use plain flaked almonds instead. If using butter cream instead of the vanilla frosting, you will need one quantity of butter cream (see page 110).

starting the night shift

TAKES OVER 1 HOUR

You will need 1 x 20cm (8-inch) round cake for this recipe.

EQUIPMENT

25cm (10-inch) round cake board

5cm (2-inch) round cutter

3cm (1¼-inch) round cutter

2cm (¾-inch) round cutter

CAKE

½ x 460g (14½ ounce) packaged double unfilled sponge cake rounds

½ x 453g (14½-ounce) tub vanilla frosting

½ x 453g (14½-ounce) tub dark chocolate frosting

DECORATIONS

1 x 110g (3½ ounces) packet natural flaked almonds (skin on)

50g (1½ ounces) ready-made white icing

pure icing (confectioners') sugar, for dusting

orange food colouring

1 black round jube, halved

1 Secure cake to the cake board with a little frosting. Mark two large semi circles on the cake, leaving a 5cm (2-inch) gap between the circles (this is where the chocolate frosting will go). Spread the vanilla frosting between the marked lines over the top and sides of the cake (where the almonds will go).

2 Spread chocolate frosting over the remaining top and side of cake.

3 Using picture as a guide, decorate vanilla frosted part of the cake with almonds.

4 Knead ready-made icing on a surface dusted with a little icing sugar until icing loses its stickiness. Roll three-quarters of the icing on a surface dusted with icing sugar into a 3mm (⅛-inch) thickness (see page 114). Using the 5cm and 3cm cutters, cut two of each sized circle from icing. Secure smaller circle to larger circle with a tiny amount of water. Position on cake for eyes.

5 Tint remaining ready-made icing orange. Roll on a surface dusted with a little icing sugar into a 3mm (⅛-inch) thickness. Using the 2cm cutter, cut two circles from icing; cut a 4cm (1½-inch) diamond from remaining icing. Position orange circles on top of white circles with a tiny amount of water. Position diamond on centre of cake for owl's beak.

6 Secure black jubes on orange circles with a little frosting for pupils. Roll a little remaining white icing into small balls, flatten slightly; secure to black jubes with a little water, as pictured.

puppy dogs' tales

TAKES UP TO 1 HOUR

EQUIPMENT

30cm x 40cm (12-inch x 16-inch) rectangular cake board

large plastic lunch bag or piping bag

CAKE

1 x 500g (1-pound) double chocolate sponge roll

2 x 453g (14½-ounce) tubs dark chocolate frosting

5 chocolate rollettes

DECORATIONS

2 blue M&M's

2 white chocolate Melts

6 blue mini M&M's

6 Milky Bar buttons

1 red M&M

3 red mini M&M's

1 red sour strap

1 Secure the sponge roll to the cake board with a little frosting. Using a small knife, cut one chocolate rollette in half crossways; trim one half until it is slightly rounded, discard remaining half. Secure rollette to one end of the sponge roll with a little frosting to form a nose.

2 Secure three chocolate rollettes to the cake board with a little frosting. Trim remaining rollette into 1.5cm (¾-inch) cubes; secure to one end of each rollette with a little frosting to form little noses for the puppies.

3 Spoon frosting into a large plastic bag or piping bag. Use scissors to snip a small opening in the corner of the bag. Pipe frosting in long lines, back and forth over the bodies of the dog and puppies, extending over back end and piping over noses, as pictured.

4 Using a little frosting, secure blue M&Ms to the white Melts; repeat with blue mini M&M's and the Milky Bar buttons. Secure Melts on the large dog for eyes and Milky Bar buttons on puppies. Pipe the remaining frosting around the eyes to create a fringe.

5 Secure a red M&M on the dog for a nose and the red mini M&M's on the puppies for noses. Use kitchen scissors to trim the sour strap into a 4cm (1½-inch) long tongue for the dog; attach tongue under the nose.

test kitchen tips

The sponge roll used for this recipe
has a diameter of 10cm (4-inches)
and a length of 16cm (6½-inches).
Brush the sour strap with a little
water to remove the sugar crystals.

test kitchen tips

Colour the jelly pale blue. We used
create-a-jelly (available from larger
supermarkets), which are clear jelly
crystals that you add your own
flavours and colours to, this way you
can control the depth of the colour.
You can use blue or green jelly
crystals, if you like, but it will be
darker in colour and you may not be
able to see the details in the fish bowl
as well. Allow yourself plenty of time
so the jelly can set between stages.

life in a fish bowl

TAKES OVER 1 HOUR (+ REFRIGERATION & FREEZING)

A no-cake birthday cake! Start making this jelly cake 6 hours ahead of the party to allow the jelly time to set.

EQUIPMENT

1-litre (4-cup) glass bowl

CAKE

4 x 85g (3-ounce) packets create-a-jelly crystals

blue food colouring

DECORATIONS

30 yellow jubes

4 drained canned apricot halves

2 red sour straps

2 dark choc Bits

15 green rainbow laces

¼ teaspoon hundreds and thousands

1 Position jubes in base of glass bowl. Make one packet of jelly following packet directions; tint pale blue. Pour enough jelly into the glass bowl to just cover the jubes (you don't want them to float). Refrigerate until jelly is set.

2 To make fish, place two apricot halves together; place on a small oven tray. Cut sour strap into fin shapes; push in between apricot halves to secure. Gently push a choc Bit into apricot for an eye. Repeat with remaining apricots, sour strap and choc Bit; freeze for 1 hour or until firm.

3 Tie bunches of rainbow laces together, knotting at one end. Push laces into jelly, making sure they are firmly in place. Make remaining three jellies following packet directions; tint pale blue. Pour jelly into bowl (the sour straps may float up, but should be anchored at the base to form seaweed). Refrigerate for 1 hour or until nearly set.

4 When the jelly is almost set, push the fish into the jelly with the eye up against the glass. Refrigerate until jelly is completely set. Sprinkle top of jelly with hundreds and thousands as fish food.

myrtle the turtle

TAKES OVER 1 HOUR MAKES 12

½ x 453g (14½-ounce) tub dark chocolate frosting

3 x 460g (14½-ounce) packets muffins

24 each green and purple soft square or diamond jubes, cut in half crossways

30 spearmint leaves

12 green oval jubes

24 blue mini M&M's

1 Spread frosting over cake tops.
2 Using picture as a guide, decorate cake tops with the jubes to make a tortoise shell pattern. Position mint leaves for legs and tail, and oval jubes for head. Secure two M&M's to each head for eyes with a little frosting.

tips If using butter cream for these recipes instead of frosting, you will need to make half a quantity of butter cream (see page 110); tint it the colour(s) required by the recipe. Packaged cupcakes usually come iced, however, you can ice over the top with the frosting or remove the icing. Place the muffins in matching paper cases, if you like.

nippy the crab

TAKES OVER 1 HOUR (+ STANDING) MAKES 12

½ x 453g (14½-ounce) tub vanilla frosting

orange food colouring

3 x 460g (14½-ounce) packets muffins

½ cup (75g) white chocolate Melts

12 ice-cream wafer biscuits

¼ cup orange sprinkles

24 brown mini M&M's

24 oval orange jubes

6 yellow rectangle jubes, sliced thinly

5cm (2-inch) round cutter

1 Tint frosting orange; spread over cake tops.
2 Melt chocolate (see page 115). Use the cutter to cut a round from each wafer. Lay the rounds on a piece of baking paper, spread with melted chocolate; sprinkle with sprinkles. Stand until set.
3 Secure two mini M&M's to the rounds for eyes with a little melted chocolate; stand until set.
4 Cut a small 'V' shape from the top of each orange jube for claws. Using picture as a guide, place the chocolate rounds on top of each cupcake. Secure two jubes for claws and sliced yellow jubes for legs.

leggit the octopus

TAKES OVER 1 HOUR (+ STANDING) **MAKES** 12

½ x 453g (14½-ounce) tub vanilla frosting

½ cup (75g) white chocolate Melts

yellow and green food colouring

3 x 460g (14½-ounce) packets muffins

12 ice-cream wafer biscuits

¼ cup green sprinkles

12 white mini marshmallows, halved

24 brown mini M&M's

12 or 48 rainbow sour straps (see tip next column)

5cm (2-inch) round cutter

1 Tint frosting yellow; spread over cake tops.

2 Melt chocolate (see page 115); tint green. To make heads, cut a round from each wafer; lay on a piece of baking paper. Spread wafers with chocolate, sprinkle with green sprinkles. Stand until set.

3 Secure marshmallows and M&M's to wafers with a little melted chocolate for eyes; stand until set.

4 If using green-only legs, cut green strips from straps, cut in half crossways. Repeat until you have 96 legs. Using picture as a guide, place heads upright on top of the cakes; secure 8 legs around each cake.

snapper the shark

TAKES OVER 1 HOUR (+ STANDING) **MAKES** 12

1 x 453g (14½-ounce) tub vanilla frosting

blue and black food colouring

3 x 460g (14½-ounce) packets muffins

12 ice-cream wafer biscuits

5cm (2-inch) round cutter

1 Divide frosting in half. Tint half the frosting blue; spread over cake tops. Add 1 teaspoon of reserved frosting to the top of each cupcake; swirl the colours to look like waves.

2 Using the cutter, cut a round from each wafer. Make another cut in the round to form the shape of a shark's fin (with a pointy piece on the bottom to push into the cupcake).

3 Tint remaining frosting grey with black food colouring. Lay the shark fins on a piece of baking paper; spread with grey frosting. Carefully push shark fins into the centre of each cupcake.

leggit the octopus tip To get 96 green legs you need a total of 48 strips of rainbow sour strap, however, if you give the octopus multi-coloured legs, you will only need 12 rainbow straps. Cut the straps in half, and cut the colours into strips.

never smile at a crocodile

TAKES OVER 1 HOUR (+ REFRIGERATION)

You will need 3 sponge slabs for this recipe.

EQUIPMENT

35cm x 45cm (14-inch x 17½-inch) large shallow plastic tray

CAKE

1 x 85g (3-ounce) packet blueberry jelly

1½ x 450g (14½-ounce) packaged double unfilled sponge slabs

2 x 453g (14½-ounce) tubs vanilla frosting

green food colouring

DECORATIONS

3 x 300g (9½-ounce) packets spearmint leaves, halved

6 teeth lollies

2 brown M&M's

1 white marshmallow, halved crossways

1cm (½-inch) piece licorice twist, halved crossways

4 white milk bottles

1 Make jelly following packet instructions. Pour into tray; refrigerate 1 hour or until set.

2 Position cakes, side-by-side, short ends together. Using a small serrated knife, trim the cakes into a crocodile shape. Use cake off-cuts to make legs. Position cakes on jelly.

3 Tint frosting green; carefully spread frosting all over top and sides of cake.

4 Using picture as a guide, position mint leaves, cut-side up, over crocodile's body.

5 Using kitchen scissors, cut small wedges from the teeth lollies to create pointy teeth; position around mouth. Secure two M&M's on the end of the nose for nostrils. Secure marshmallow on the top of the head for eyes, then attach the licorice slices with a little frosting for pupils.

6 Cut tops from milk bottles; cut each milk bottle into three lengthways. Position on legs as claws.

test kitchen tips
If you don't like spearmint leaves,
use green racing car lollies or green
jubes for scales as an alternative.
If using butter cream instead
of the vanilla frosting, you will
need 2 quantities of butter cream
(see page 110).

test kitchen tips

Add a ready-made icing bow to the ear for a girly elephant or use a pretty ribbon. If using butter cream instead of the vanilla frosting, you will need one quantity of butter cream (see page 110).

flutter-by pops

TAKES UP TO 1 HOUR
(+ REFRIGERATION & STANDING) **MAKES** 12

1 cup (150g) dark chocolate Melts

100g (3 ounces) mini marshmallows

½ cup (120g) raspberry lollies, chopped

12 lollipop sticks

12 mini paper cases (see tip)

1 tablespoon butterfly sprinkles

1 Melt chocolate (see page 115).
2 Combine marshmallows, raspberry lollies and three-quarters of the melted chocolate in a medium bowl; spoon a rounded teaspoonful of mixture into the mini paper cases. Decorate with sprinkles. Refrigerate until set.
3 Dip the end of one lollipop stick into the melted chocolate (re-melt if necessary); push about halfway into the marshmallow mixture. Stand upright in a styrofoam block (see page 111) until set.

tips Cut the paper cases so they resemble grass, if you like. Pierce the bottom of the paper case with a metal skewer before inserting the lollypop stick.

magical mushrooms

TAKES OVER 1 HOUR (+ STANDING) **MAKES** 12

375g (12-ounce) packet white chocolate Melts

12 domed white marshmallows

36 pink (musk) life savers

12 lollipop sticks

6 strawberry sour straws, sliced thinly

1 Melt chocolate (see page 115).
2 Dip the end of one lollipop stick into the melted chocolate; push about halfway into a marshmallow. Repeat with remaining sticks and marshmallows. Stand upright in a styrofoam block (see page 111) until set.
3 Dip one marshmallow into the melted chocolate (re-melt if necessary), rocking back and forth to coat (don't swirl the pop or it will fall off). Allow excess chocolate to drip back into the jug. Using picture as a guide, thread three life savers onto the bottom of the pop, securing with a little melted chocolate. Stand upright in a styrofoam block until set.
4 Secure sour straw pieces to tops of mushrooms with a little melted chocolate.

test kitchen tips

Add licorice eyelashes to make Milly Monkey, if you like; just cut into a piece of licorice strap to make the lashes. If using butter cream instead of the frostings, you need one quantity of butter cream (see page 110). Add 1½ tablespoons sifted cocoa to half the mixture to make chocolate butter cream.

monkey business

TAKES UP TO 1 HOUR

EQUIPMENT

30cm (14-inch) round cake board

disposable plastic piping bag or
plastic lunch bag

CAKE

1 x 600g (1¼-ounce) packaged round chocolate
mud cake

2 x 115g (3½-ounce) large blueberry muffins

½ x 453g (14½-ounce) tub dark chocolate frosting

½ x 453g (14½-ounce) tub vanilla frosting

DECORATIONS

2 orange Smarties

10cm (4-inch) thin piece black licorice strap

2 large chocolate coins

1 white marshmallow, halved crossways

2 blue Smarties

2 ice-cream wafers

1 Secure cake to the cake board with a little frosting. Cut 2cm (¾-inch) from the base of the muffins; reserve one of the off-cuts. Trim 2cm (¾-inch) lengthways off each muffin. Secure muffins to cake, with a little frosting to form ears. Spread top and sides of cake and muffins with chocolate frosting.

2 Position muffin off-cut on cake for nose. Place vanilla icing in a piping bag; snip a medium opening in one corner. Using picture as a guide, pipe over nose and pipe two large circles on cake to form eyes; smooth frosting. Position orange Smarties and licorice on muffin to form nose and mouth.

3 Top eyes with chocolate coins; secure marshmallow and blue Smarties to coins with a little frosting.

4 Trim wafers, using picture as a guide; position wafers on ears.

here kitty kitty

TAKES OVER 1 HOUR

EQUIPMENT

30cm (14-inch) round cake board

4cm (1½-inch) round cutter

1cm (½-inch) round cutter

CAKE

1 x 600g (1¼-ounce) round chocolate mud cake

1 x 115g (3½-ounce) large blueberry muffin

½ x 453g (14½-ounce) tub vanilla frosting

orange and blue food colouring

20g (¾ ounce) ready-made white icing

pure icing (confectioners') sugar, for dusting

DECORATIONS

20cm (8-inch) piece black licorice strap

1 pink marshmallow, halved crossways

1 red sour strap

1 fruit salad roll up

2 strawberries and cream lollies

1 Secure cake to the cake board with a little frosting. Cut muffin in quarters. Trim round side of two muffin pieces into triangles; secure to the cake with a little frosting to form the ears. Discard the remaining muffin pieces.

2 Tint frosting orange. Spread over top and sides of cake.

3 Knead ready-made icing on a surface dusted with a little sifted icing sugar until icing loses its stickiness. Tint half the icing blue.

4 Roll white icing on a surface dusted with a little icing sugar into a 3mm (⅛-inch) thickness (see page 114). Using the 4cm cutter, cut two rounds from icing. Roll blue icing on a surface dusted with a little icing sugar into a 3mm thickness. Using the 1cm cutter, cut two rounds from icing. Secure blue rounds to white rounds with a little water to form eyes; position on cake. Cut two small strips of licorice; secure to eyes with a little water, for pupils.

5 Secure marshmallow on centre of the cake for the nose. Cut licorice into two thin strips; position on cake to form mouth. Shape a 4cm (1½-inch) piece of sour strap into a tongue shape, secure to cake. Cut 6 x 3mm (⅛-inch) thin strips from the yellow part of the roll up; position on cake to form whiskers.

6 Discard the red section from the strawberries and cream lollies; position white part as ears, as pictured. Decorate the cake with a bow if you like (see page 115 for instructions).

test kitchen tip

If using butter cream instead of the vanilla frosting, you will need one quantity of butter cream (see page 110).

test kitchen tips

Macaroons are available from speciality bakery shops and select supermarkets. If you can't find them, any small round filled biscuit will do. Try mini Oreos or mini Wagon Wheels, or Monte Carlos. If using butter cream instead of the vanilla frosting, you will need one quantity of butter cream (see page 110).

olivia longneck

TAKES OVER 1 HOUR

EQUIPMENT

30cm x 50cm (14-inch x 20-inch) rectangular cake board

CAKE

1 x 600g (1¼-ounce) round chocolate mud cake

1 x 115g (3½-ounce) large chocolate muffin

1 x 453g (14½-ounce) tub dark chocolate frosting

DECORATIONS

2 x 200g (6½ ounce) packets Venetian biscuits

½ cup (50g) shredded coconut

1 ice-cream wafer

½ white marshmallow

½ round black jube

1 mint Tic Tac

8 yellow macaroons (see tips)

2 banana lollies, halved lengthways

15 chocolate finger biscuits

1 Secure cake to the cake board with a little frosting. Spread frosting over top and side of cake.

2 Using picture as a guide, build the emu's neck with Venetian biscuits, securing them together with a little frosting.

3 Position the muffin at the top of the neck for the head; secure with a little frosting. Spread top and side with frosting.

4 Using picture as a guide, decorate head and body with coconut.

5 Cut one wafer into two triangles; position on head for beak. Position marshmallow on head for eye, top with jube and Tic Tac; secure with a little frosting.

6 Using picture as a guide, build the emu's leg with macaroons, attaching them together with a little frosting. Position three pieces of bananas for claws.

7 Position finger biscuits on the board at the back of the emu's body to resemble tail feathers.

PRETTY
IN PINK

minty sunrise cake

TAKES UP TO 1 HOUR

EQUIPMENT

30cm (12-inch) round cake board

CAKE

1 x 460g (14½-ounce) packaged double unfilled sponge cake rounds

1 x 453g (14½-ounce) tub cream-cheese frosting

DECORATIONS

9 x 37.5g (1¼-ounce) packets rainbow Mentos, approximately (see tips)

9 x 37.5g (1¼-ounce) packets fruit Mentos, approximately (see tips)

1 Level cake tops. Secure one cake to the cake board with a little frosting. Spread top of cake with ⅓ cup of frosting, top with remaining cake. Spread top and side of cake with remaining frosting.

2 Divide lollies into colours. Using picture as a guide, secure Mentos around side of the cake.

test kitchen tips

To decorate the cake in the same colours as pictured here, you need 32 of each colour. We used rainbow Mentos mints, which come in packs of three. The purple and green colours can be used in lolly bags. Decorate the cake however you like using all the colours, rather than the ones used here. If using butter cream instead of cream-cheese frosting, you will need one quantity of butter cream coloured pale yellow (see page 110).

test kitchen tips

For a boy, decorate with green or yellow fruit sticks and matching bunting, or use the colours of his favourite sporting team (of course, this also can be done for girls and their favourite team). If using butter cream instead of the strawberry frosting, you need one quantity of butter cream tinted pale pink (see page 110).

little baby bunting

TAKES UP TO 1 HOUR

EQUIPMENT

30cm (12-inch) round cake board

CAKE

2 x 600g (1¼-pound) white chocolate mud cakes, icing removed

1 x 453g (14½-ounce) tub strawberry frosting

DECORATIONS

3 x 200g (6½-ounce) packets musk sticks

1½m (1½ yards) miniature bunting

small wooden toothpicks

2 x 25cm (10-inch) painted sticks

1 Level cake tops. Secure one cake to the cake board with a little frosting; spread cake top with ⅓ cup frosting. Top with the other cake. Spread all over with remaining frosting.

2 Trim musk sticks so they sit 5mm (¼-inch) above the cake. Position musk sticks around side of cake. Secure bunting around cake using toothpicks to hold bunting in place.

3 Secure bunting to sticks; push sticks into cake, as pictured.

tips The bunting can be found at most craft and party shops. Be sure to remove the toothpicks from the cake before serving.

fairy princess birthday cake

TAKES OVER 1 HOUR (+ REFRIGERATION)

EQUIPMENT

20cm (8-inch) round cardboard cake board

10cm (4-inch) round cardboard cake board

30cm (12-inch) round cake board

10cm (4-inch) round cutter

CAKE

3 x 600g (1¼-pound) packaged white chocolate mud cakes

2 quantities white chocolate ganache (see page 110)

DECORATIONS

2 x 190g (6-ounce) packets natural coloured hundreds and thousands

1½m (1 yard) x 4cm (1½-inch) wide pink striped ribbon

1 Level cake tops. Split all cakes in half. Secure one round to the 20cm cake board. Spread with ⅓ cup ganache; top with another half cake. Repeat with ganache and another cake round (so there are three half cakes sandwiched with ganache).

2 Cut 10cm circles from the remaining three cake halves. Secure one cake round onto the 10cm cake board. Spread with ¼ cup ganache; top with another cake round. Repeat with ganache and remaining cake round.

3 Pour hundreds and thousands into a shallow baking tray. Spread sides of cakes with ganache. Hold cakes by the top and bottom and roll in the hundreds and thousands, making sure that all the ganache is covered (see page 113).

4 Secure the larger cake to the 30cm cake board with a little ganache. Spread the tops of both cakes with ganache; sprinkle the remaining hundreds and thousands over cake tops, ensuring all the ganache is covered. Refrigerate for 30 minutes or until firm.

5 Carefully spread a little ganache on top of the large cake in the centre; place the smaller cake on top (this helps to secure the two cakes together if it is to be transported). Tie the ribbon around the base of the top cake with a bow (see page 115 for instructions). Decorate cake with a number (such as the age of the child), if you like.

test kitchen tip

Use regular hundreds and thousands for a brighter, less pastel, cake.

test kitchen tip

For an even faster cake, buy
a variety of iced doughnuts
in different colours, and secure
them together with a little of
the vanilla frosting.

doughnut stack

TAKES UP TO 30 MINUTES

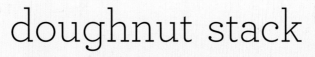

EQUIPMENT

25cm (10-inch) round cake board

wire rack

oven tray

CAKE

12 cinnamon doughnuts

1 x 453g (14½-ounce) tub vanilla frosting

pink and green food colouring

DECORATIONS

⅓ cup (65g) white sprinkles

⅓ cup (65g) pink sprinkles

1 Place doughnuts on a wire rack over an oven tray. Divide frosting among two microwave-safe bowls; tint one pink and one green.

2 Heat pink frosting in a microwave oven on HIGH (100%) for 15 seconds or until frosting is of a runny consistency. Spoon frosting over half the doughnuts. Repeat with green frosting and remaining doughnuts. Decorate pink doughnuts with white sprinkles and green doughnuts with pink sprinkles.

3 Stack doughnuts on a cake stand or cake board.

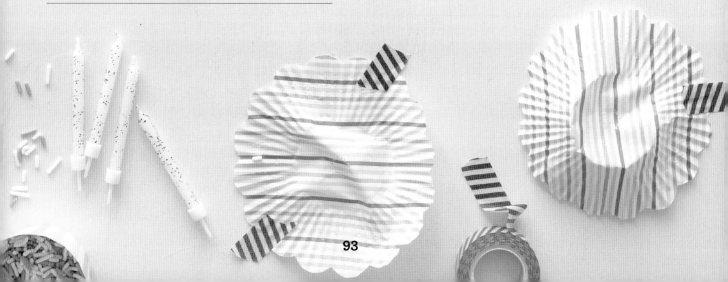

93

minty raspberry ice-cream cake

TAKES OVER 1 HOUR (+ FREEZING)

Make this cake the day before the party to allow the ice-cream layers time to set. You only need one round sponge for this recipe.

EQUIPMENT

18cm (7¼-inch) (closed base measurement) round springform pan

25cm (10-inch) serving plate or cake stand

CAKE

½ x 460g (14½-ounce) packaged double unfilled sponge cake rounds

⅓ cup (80ml) strawberry topping

2-litres (8-cups) vanilla ice-cream, softened

pink and green food colouring

½ cup (90g) raspberry lollies, chopped coarsely

½ cup (110g) spearmint leaves, chopped coarsely

½ x 453g (14½-ounce) tub strawberry frosting

DECORATIONS

6 assorted icing flowers

2 spearmint leaves, halved

1 Line base and sides of pan with plastic wrap, allowing a 5cm (2-inch) overhang.

2 Split the cake in half; brush the cut sides with strawberry topping. Place one cake half, topping-side up, in the base of the pan.

3 Divide ice-cream evenly among three bowls. Return two bowls to the freezer while working with the third bowl.

4 Tint bowl of ice-cream pink; add raspberries, stir to combine. Spoon over cake; smooth surface. Freeze 20 minutes or until just firm.

5 Remove the second bowl of ice-cream from the freezer to soften slightly. Spoon vanilla ice-cream over the pink ice-cream; smooth the surface. Freeze 20 minutes or until just firm.

6 Remove the last bowl of ice-cream from the freezer to soften slightly. Tint ice-cream green; add the spearmint leaves, stir to combine. Spoon over the vanilla ice-cream; smooth the surface. Top with the remaining cake layer, cut-side down.

7 Loosely cover ice-cream cake with plastic wrap. Freeze for 4 hours or overnight until firm. Remove from pan; place on serving plate. Spread frosting over cake top; decorate with flowers and mint leaves.

test kitchen tips

Remove each bowl from the freezer for 5 minutes before you are ready to use it to soften the ice-cream slightly. You could buy a tub of neapolitan ice-cream and divide the flavours into separate bowls to soften; add the mint leaves to the chocolate ice-cream for a choc-mint flavour.

test kitchen tips

Use any shaped cutter for this cake: try snowflakes or stars. You can use letter cutters and write the name of the child on the cake. Use coloured sprinkles that suit the occasion of your party. If using butter cream instead of the strawberry frosting, you will need one quantity of butter cream coloured pale pink (see page 110).

princess of hearts

TAKES UP TO 1 HOUR

EQUIPMENT

25cm x 35cm (10-inch x 14-inch) rectangular cake board

5cm (2-inch) heart cutter

3cm (1¼-inch) heart cutter

CAKE

1 x 450g (14½-ounce) packaged double unfilled sponge slabs

1 x 453g (14½-ounce) tub strawberry frosting

DECORATIONS

1 tablespoon pink pearl sprinkles

1 tablespoon white pearl sprinkles

1 Trim edges of cakes; split each cake in half. Secure one cake layer to the cake board with a little frosting; spread a third of the frosting over the cake, sandwich with another cake layer. Repeat with another third of the frosting and one more cake layer. (Discard or reserve the remaining cake slab for another use). Spread remaining frosting over top of cake.

2 Place heart cutters, one at a time, on the frosting. Sprinkle ½ teaspoon sprinkles to cover the inside of the cutter. Use the back of a teaspoon to lightly press the sprinkles into the frosting to secure. Gently lift the cutter, being careful not to spread sprinkles outside of the heart shape. Repeat with remaining sprinkles to decorate the cake with hearts.

macaroon munch

TAKES UP TO 30 MINUTES

EQUIPMENT

30cm (12-inch) round cake board

CAKE

2 x 600g (1¼-pound) packaged chocolate mud cakes

2 quantities white chocolate ganache (see page 110)

DECORATIONS

7 x 144g (4½-ounce) packets macaroons

1 Level top of cakes to remove icing. Secure one cake to the cake board with a little ganache. Spread cake top with ⅓ cup of ganache; top with remaining cake. Spread top and side of cake with remaining ganache.
2 Using picture as a guide, decorate the cake all over with macaroons.

test kitchen tips

Macaroons are available from specialty bakery shops and select supermarkets. We used ganache to cover the cake as it will set and hold the macaroons in place. We bought 15 packets of macaroons to get the 30 pink, 6 brown, 19 vanilla and 18 light brown colours used in this cake. To save money, use all the colours in the packets to make a rainbow cake.

whimsical meringue cake

TAKES UP TO 30 MINUTES

EQUIPMENT

25cm (10-inch) round cake board

CAKE

2 x 600g (1¼-pound) packaged chocolate mud cakes

1 x 453g (14½-ounce) tub vanilla frosting

DECORATIONS

2 x 100g (3-ounces) packets mini rainbow meringues

1 Level tops of cakes to remove icing. Secure one cake to the cake board with a little frosting. Spread top of cake with ⅓ cup of frosting; top with the remaining cake. Spread top and side of cake with remaining frosting.

2 Secure meringues around the side and top of the cake.

test kitchen tips

You can make your own meringues for this cake and colour them any colour you like. This works well as a Christmas cake using green and white meringues. If using butter cream instead of the vanilla frosting, you will need one quantity of butter cream coloured pale yellow (see page 110).

wildfire flower cake

TAKES OVER 1 HOUR

EQUIPMENT

30cm x 40cm (12-inch x 16-inch) rectangular cake board

CAKE

1 x 450g (14½-ounce) packaged double unfilled sponge slabs

1 x 453g (14½-ounce) tub vanilla frosting

DECORATIONS

7 red snakes

14 spearmint leaves, halved

7 creamy yellow Jelly Belly beans, halved

3 red Jelly Belly beans, halved

4 orange Jelly Belly beans, halved

3 pale pink Jelly Belly beans, halved

1 bright yellow Jelly Belly bean, halved

3 red square jubes, halved

2 yellow square jubes, halved

4 each orange and red oval jubes, halved

4 pale pink square jubes, halved

2 pink oval jubes, halved

3 purple rectangle jubes, halved

5 each yellow and orange rectangle jubes, halved

9 red rectangle jubes, halved

1 orange oval jube

1 green snake, sliced thinly

2 teaspoons rainbow nerds

1 Secure cakes, side-by-side, to cake board with a little frosting; spread top and sides with frosting.
2 Tie red snakes into knots; trim tails, discard (or eat) tails. Using picture as a guide, decorate cake top with knotted snake heads, spearmint leaves, jelly beans, jubes and nerds to make flower patterns on cake. Use the thinly sliced green snakes to make stems and tendrils.

test kitchen tips

If using butter cream instead of the vanilla frosting, you will need one quantity of butter cream (see page 110). We used a variety of different jubes to get different shapes.

test kitchen tips

You could fill the cones with scoops of ice-cream instead of the cupcakes just before serving. Tint the frosting a colour to match your party theme. If using butter cream instead of the vanilla frosting, you will need one quantity of butter cream (see page 110).

ice-cream cone cake

TAKES UP TO 1 HOUR

EQUIPMENT

30cm (12-inch) round cake board

CAKE

2 x 600g (1¼-pound) packaged chocolate mud cakes

½ x 453g (14½-ounce) tub vanilla frosting

DECORATIONS

8 flat-bottomed ice-cream cones

8 x 20g (¾-ounce) mini iced cupcakes

½m (1 yard) x 2½cm (1-inch) wide pink and white striped ribbon

1 Level top of cakes to remove icing. Secure one cake to the cake board with a little frosting. Spread top of cake with ⅓ cup of frosting, top with remaining cake. Spread top and side of cake with remaining frosting.

2 Reserve 3 cones. Using a sharp serrated knife, cut remaining ice-cream cones in half lengthways.

3 Remove cupcakes from paper cases. Reserve 3 cakes; cut remaining cakes in half lengthways.

4 Position a halved cupcake in each cone half. Using picture as a guide, secure cones halves around cake. Place reserved cakes in reserved cones; position on top of cake. Secure ribbon around cake (see page 115 for instructions on making a bow).

jam roll of hearts

TAKES UP TO 30 MINUTES

EQUIPMENT

40cm (16-inch) square cake board

CAKE

4 x 250g (8-ounce) packets jam rollettes, halved

DECORATIONS

1 tablespoon icing (confectioners') sugar

1 Using picture as a guide, position jam rollettes on the cake board to form a heart shape. Lightly dust with sifted icing sugar.

test kitchen tip

Use assorted cream-filled rollettes for a colourful alternative.

into the fairy forest

TAKES UP TO 30 MINUTES

EQUIPMENT

20cm x 25cm (8-inch x 10-inch) rectangular
cake board

CAKE

1 x 500g (1-pound) honey sponge roll

1 x 238g (7½-ounce) can petal pink soft frosting

DECORATIONS

2 x 16g (½-ounce) packet pansy icing flowers

½ x 19g (¾-ounce) packet rose icing flowers

1 Secure cake to the cake board with a little frosting.
Place the fluted nozzle on the icing can and pipe
rosettes all over the top and sides of cake.
2 Decorate with icing flowers.

test kitchen tip

You can use a tub of strawberry frosting,
if you prefer; place the frosting in a piping
bag fitted with a small fluted tube to pipe
the rosettes.

little shop of cupcakes

TAKES UP TO 1 HOUR

EQUIPMENT

30cm (12-inch) square cake board

12 yellow mini paper cases

CAKE

1 x 450g (14½-ounce) packaged double unfilled sponge slabs

1 x 453g (14½-ounce) tub strawberry frosting

DECORATIONS

12 mini iced cupcakes

1 Secure one cake to the cake board with a little frosting. Spread top with ⅓ cup of the frosting.

2 Cut one-third from the long side of the remaining cake; reserve both cake pieces.

3 Position the larger cake piece on top of the cake on the cake board, so the backs of the cakes are aligned. Spread top with ¼ cup of frosting.

4 Position the remaining cake piece on top so all cakes are aligned to create 'steps'. Spread top and sides of cake with remaining frosting.

5 Place cupcakes into paper cases; position along the steps.

test kitchen tip

If using butter cream instead of the strawberry frosting, you will need one quantity of butter cream tinted pink (see page 110).

test kitchen tips

Use strawberry or chocolate flavoured ice-cream instead of the vanilla. Use any lollies you like in the ice-cream: if they are large, roughly chop them. Make this a rocky road ice-cream sandwich by adding chopped turkish delight, dark choc chips, peanuts and coconut.

ice-cream sandwiches

TAKES OVER 1 HOUR (+ FREEZING)

Make this cake the day before the party to allow the ice-cream sandwiches time to firm up.

EQUIPMENT

20cm x 30cm (8-inch x 12-inch) rectangular cake pan

2 oven trays

7.5cm (3-inch) round cutter

CAKE

2-litres (8-cups) vanilla ice-cream, softened

1 x 180g (5½-ounce) packet Smarties

1 x 450g (14½ ounce) packet ready-to-bake M&M's cookie dough

1 Grease cake pan; line base and sides with baking paper, extending paper 5cm (2-inches) above sides.
2 Place ice-cream in a large bowl. Gently fold in Smarties. Spoon mixture into pan; smooth surface. Freeze for 2 hours or overnight until firm.
3 Preheat oven to 180°C/350°F. Grease and line oven trays with baking paper.
4 Cut cookie dough into 16 x 1cm (½-inch) thick slices; place 2cm (¾-inch) apart on trays. Bake for 10 minutes or until golden brown. Cool on trays.
5 Cut eight rounds from ice-cream using round cutter; sandwich each round between 2 cookies. Place on a tray; freeze for 30 minutes or overnight until firm.

ICING RECIPES

Butter cream

Basic butter cream is also known as vienna cream; the flavour can be varied by adding any extract or essence you like.

125g (4 ounces) unsalted butter, softened

1½ cups (240g) icing sugar (confectioners' sugar)

2 tablespoons milk

Beat the butter in a small bowl with an electric mixer until as white as possible. Gradually beat in half the sifted icing sugar, milk, then remaining icing sugar.
(See how to colour and cover a cake with butter cream, page 112.)

Chocolate variation: Sift ⅓ cup (35g) cocoa powder in with the first batch of icing sugar.

Ready-made white icing

Ready-made icing is available from cake-decorating suppliers and supermarkets. There are several brands available. This is very easy to use. Break off as much icing as you need; re-wrap remaining icing to exclude the air or a crust will develop, which will spoil the smooth texture of the icing. Knead the icing on a surface lightly dusted with sifted icing sugar. If colouring the icing, start working tiny amounts of the colouring through the icing. The icing should be smooth and free from stickiness. Only work with small amounts of icing at a time as the air will dry it out. Cover any rolled-out icing with plastic wrap.
To cover a cake with the icing, use the rolling pin to lift the icing onto the cake. Lightly dust hands with icing sugar and gently mould and smooth the icing around the shape of the cake. Trim excess icing away from around the edge of the cake. (See how to roll and cover a cake with ready-made icing, page 114.)

Ganache

Ganache is a mixture of melted chocolate and cream. It is wonderfully simple to make and versatile to use. It can be used while it's still warm as a glaze over a cake. Or, let the ganache partly set, either at a cool room temperature or in the refrigerator, then beat it with a wooden spoon until it's spreadable – making it a perfect filling or frosting. Ganache can be refrigerated for around 30 minutes, or until it becomes thick and spreadable, then whipped with an electric mixer until it increases in volume and becomes fluffy, making it ideal for a frosting or filling.

Ganache will keep in the refrigerator, covered tightly, for about two weeks (stand at room temperature to soften before use), or frozen for 3 months; thaw overnight in the refrigerator, or thaw it in the microwave oven, using short bursts of power.

White Chocolate Ganache

360g (11½ ounces) white chocolate

½ cup (125ml) pouring cream

1 Break chocolate into food processor; process until chocolate is finely chopped.
2 Bring cream to the boil in a small saucepan; remove from heat.
3 Add chocolate to cream; stir until ganache is smooth.
4 Cool mixture to room temperature if not being used as a glaze (in which case use while warm and pourable) before beating or whipping to the desired consistency.
MAKES ENOUGH TO COVER A DEEP 20CM (8-INCH) ROUND CAKE.

Colouring butter cream: Use a skewer to dab a tiny amount of colouring onto the butter cream, mix the colouring through thoroughly before adding any more.

Whipping ganache: Cool the ganache in the fridge for around 30 minutes, stirring occasionally. Beat the ganache with an electric mixer until light and fluffy.

For dark or milk chocolate ganache, follow the recipe for the white chocolate ganache but substitute 200g (6½ ounces) milk or dark chocolate for the white chocolate.

CAKE POPS

Decorating cake pops

Coating: We used chocolate Melts (also known as chocolate buds). Because they are made from compound chocolate, they are much easier to work with than using good quality eating chocolate, and the cake pops will keep their shape at room temperature.

Chocolate: Note that white chocolate is a creamy yellow colour; if you want a white coating, you will need to purchase Candy Melts (which are different to chocolate Melts) from cake decorating suppliers. Candy Melts are also available in colours.

Melting chocolate: You may need to re-melt the chocolate every now and again if it begins to thicken. See page 115 for instructions on how to melt chocolate.

Colourings: We recommend using paste food colourings. Add just a little at a time.

Tinting: When tinting white chocolate, remember that because you are starting with a cream-coloured base, the resulting colour may not be true. An example is rose pink colouring – it will turn a salmon pink colour when added to white chocolate. If you need to match a particular colour to your party theme, use Candy Melts.

Timing your work flow: If working with a large number of cake pops, take one batch at a time out of the freezer or fridge.

Storing cake pops

Make ahead: Most cake pops can be made at least two days before the party. Once set, most cake pops will be firm enough to place lying down, in a single layer, in an airtight container. This makes them easy to store and transport.

How to store: Store cake pops at a cool, dry room temperature. If the weather is humid, you may need to refrigerate them. If you find the cake pops are a little soft, keep them standing up in styrofoam or egg cartons and cover them with an upturned box or container to keep them dust-free.

To coat cake pops in chocolate (1): Dip the end of a cake pop (lollypop) stick into the melted chocolate; push the stick about halfway through into the ball of cake.

To coat cake pops in chocolate (2): Dip each cake pop in the melted chocolate; rock them backwards and forwards to ensure they are evenly coated. Don't swirl the pops or they'll break.

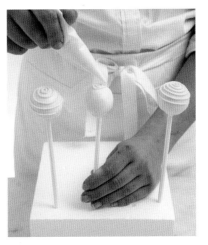

To coat cake pops in chocolate (3): Let excess chocolate drip back into the jug, then stand the cake pops in styrofoam until the coating has dried. Decorate cake pops as directed by the recipe instructions.

DECORATING TECHNIQUES

Covering a square cake board Cut the covering paper about 5cm (2 inches) larger than the board, place the board, top-side down, on the back of the paper. Use tape or glue to stick the paper to the board.

Covering a round cake board (1) Cut the covering paper about 5cm (2 inches) larger than the board, place the board, top-side down, on the back of the paper. Snip the paper border, on an angle, all the way around.

Covering a round cake board (2) Fold each snipped piece of paper over onto the board; tape or glue the paper onto the board.

Levelling cakes Many cakes need to have their domed tops cut off so that the cakes sit flat on a cake board or plate. Use a large sharp serrated knife to do this.

Colouring butter cream Use a skewer to dab a tiny amount of colouring onto the butter cream, mix the colouring through the butter cream thoroughly before adding any more.

Icing the cake (1) Using a metal spatula, apply a very thin layer of butter cream evenly over the cold cake, don't worry if crumbs become mixed with this layer of butter cream. If necessary, refrigerate or freeze the cake to set the butter cream.

Icing the cake (2) Spread the next layer of butter cream evenly over the 'undercoat'. The long metal spatula gives a very smooth, even coating to the butter cream.

Colouring coconut Place the coconut in a small bowl, and add a few drops of colouring; using gloved hands, so as not to stain your hands, rub the colouring into the coconut until it is evenly coloured. Add the colouring a drop at a time, until you get the depth of colour you want.

Preparing to decorate Many cakes are turned top-side down for decorating, though some are decorated top-side up for a domed effect. The recipe will indicate if the cake is to be turned upside down to decorate.

Cutting cake into layers (1) Use bamboo skewers as a guide for the knife to split the cake. If the cake is large, long skewers can be pushed through the cake, from one side to the other.

Cutting cake into layers (2) If the cake is small, use toothpicks to mark the layer. Use a sharp serrated knife to split the cake. Cut the cake just above the skewers or toothpicks, you should feel the knife touch the skewers as you cut through the cake.

Coating the side of a cake Have the ingredient to coat the cake in a large shallow pan – this can be nuts, hundreds and thousands or coconut, etc. Hold the cake between both hands and roll the cake like a wheel to cover the frosting.

Colouring sugar Place the sugar in a small ziptop bag, and add a few drops of food colouring. Massage the colouring into the sugar until it is evenly coloured. Add the colouring a drop at a time, until you get the depth of colour you want.

Making a paper piping bag (1) Cut a square from a sheet of baking paper, fold it in half diagonally, then cut it in half along the fold to make two triangles.

Shaping the paper piping bag (2) Hold the apex of the triangle towards you, wrap one point of the triangle around to form a cone shape; repeat with the other point, then wriggle the three points of the triangle until they line up perfectly.

Secure the paper piping bag (3) Staple the piping bag to hold the three points of the triangle in place. To use, half-fill the bag with icing, snip a tiny piece from the point of the bag, and pipe a little icing to see if the hole is large enough, if not, snip more paper from the point of the bag.

Colouring ready-made icing Always use good-quality food colourings for best results. Start with a tiny dab of the colouring and work it through the icing with your fingers. Determine the depth of the colour before adding more.

Rolling ready-made icing Roll out the icing on a surface dusted lightly with sifted icing sugar. Roll from the centre of the icing to the outside edge, turning and easing the icing to fit the cake. Do not flip the icing over to the other side.

Applying ready-made icing (1) Gently roll the icing around the rolling pin. Hold the pin with one hand while supporting the icing with the other. Lift the icing over the cake.

Applying ready-made icing (2) Lower the icing onto the cake surface, unrolling it from the rolling pin at the same time. The icing will stretch a little at this stage.

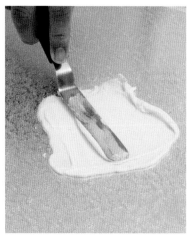

Moulding ready-made icing Lightly dust your hands with icing sugar or cornflour. Quickly smooth top of the cake, then smooth the side(s), easing the icing around the shape of the cake. Use a sharp knife to trim the excess icing from the base.

Securing cake to a cake board (1) Using a spatula, spread a dollop of butter cream, frosting or ganache on the cake board to secure the cake to the board (or plate).

Securing cake to a cake board (2) Position the cake (or a layer of a split cake) on the cake board. Gently push the cake layer into the centre of the cake board.

Securing cake to a cake board (3) If you need to stack a cake, such as we do with the fairy princess birthday cake page 90, once all cakes are on boards, secure the smaller cake to the larger cake with a little of the butter cream or frosting.

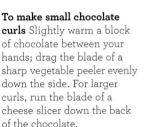

To make small chocolate curls Slightly warm a block of chocolate between your hands; drag the blade of a sharp vegetable peeler evenly down the side. For larger curls, run the blade of a cheese slicer down the back of the chocolate.

Melting chocolate Melt the chocolate in a medium heatproof bowl over a medium saucepan of simmering water, making sure that the water in the pan doesn't touch the bottom of the bowl, otherwise the chocolate will overheat and seize (turn hard and grainy). Stir until the chocolate is melted then remove from the heat.

Colouring chocolate Once the chocolate is melted add a drop or two of colour. We use paste food colours, as these don't tend to split the chocolate like water-based ones. If tinting chocolate a pastel colour, food colourings from supermarkets are fine as you only need a little, for darker more bold colours use pastes.

Piping chocolate Half-fill a paper piping bag (page 113) with melted chocolate. Fold the top of the bag over to enclose the chocolate. Cut a tiny tip off the end of bag; test to see if it is large enough for the piping you are doing, if not, carefully cut the hole a little larger.

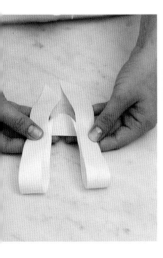

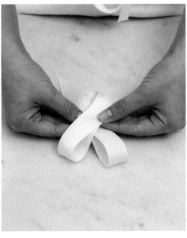

Tying a simple bow (1) Make two loops from a length of ribbon. Leave enough ribbon for tails – make these as long as you want them.

Tying a simple bow (2) Cross the loops over; bring the top loop under the bottom loop then through the hole under the bottom loop.

Tying a simple bow (3) Pull the tops of the loops at the same time to make the bow even and roughly the size you want it to be.

Tying a simple bow (4) Wriggle the loops of the bow until they are the same length, and the bow and its centre are as you want them.

GLOSSARY

BAKING PAPER (parchment paper or baking parchment) a silicone-coated paper primarily used for lining baking pans and trays so cakes and biscuits won't stick, making removal easy.

BISCUITS also known as cookies.

BUTTER use salted or unsalted (sweet) butter; 125g is equal to one stick (4oz) of butter.

CACHOUS also known as dragées; these minuscule (3mm to 5mm) metallic-looking-but-edible confectionery balls are available in silver, gold or various colours.

CAKE BOARDS often made from masonite and covered in a thick non-absorbable paper, silver or gold coloured. Come in myriad sizes, usually round or square, occasionally octagonal. If displaying on a cake board, rather than a plate, the base board is often 10-15cm larger than the cake, so it can be lifted and transported without fingers poking holes in the icing. The remaining cakes are placed on cake boards of the same size. If displaying on a cake plate, the base board should be the same size as the cake.

CHOCOLATE
dark eating also known as semi-sweet or luxury chocolate; made of a high percentage of cocoa liquor, cocoa butter, and a little added sugar.
milk mild and very sweet; similar in make-up to dark with the difference being the addition of milk solids.
white contains no cocoa solids but derives its sweet flavour from cocoa butter. Very sensitive to heat so watch carefully when melting.

COCOA POWDER also known as cocoa; dried, unsweetened, roasted and ground cocoa beans (cacao seeds).
dutch cocoa is treated with an alkali to neutralise its acids. It has a reddish-brown colour, a mild flavour and is easy to dissolve in liquids.

COCONUT
desiccated dried, unsweetened, finely shredded coconut.
essence produced from coconut flavouring, oil and alcohol.
flaked dried, flaked coconut flesh.
shredded strips of dried coconut.

CORNFLOUR (cornstarch) often used as a thickener, but can be used to roll out ready-made icing.

CREAM CHEESE commonly known as Philadelphia or Philly, a soft cow's-milk cheese with a fat content of at least 33%.

FOOD COLOURING dyes used to change the colour of foods.
concentrated pastes or gels, which is what we used throughout this book, are the easiest to use, although a little more expensive.
liquid dyes the strength varies depending on the quality. Useful for pastel colours only, as adding large amounts of liquid colouring will break down most icings. Also useful for painting icing sculptures.
powdered colourings are best for primary colours or black.

FRECKLES chocolate buttons coated on one side with coloured hundreds and thousands (nonpareils).

HUNDREDS AND THOUSANDS also known as nonpareils; tiny sugar-syrup-coated sugar crystals that come in a variety of bright colours and are used to decorate cakes and party foods.

ICE-CREAM we use full-cream ice-cream.
cones cone-shaped crisp sweet biscuit used for serving ice-cream; we used both flat-bottomed and pointy-ended cones.
wafers crisp rectangular biscuits used to serve with ice-cream.

JAM also known as preserve or conserve; most often made from fruit.

JAM ROLLETTES also known as sponge rollettes, filled with jam or jam and cream.

JELLY CRYSTALS powdered mixture of gelatine, sweetener, and artificial fruit flavouring that's used to make a moulded, translucent, quivering dessert. Also known as jello.

JUBES sugar-coated fruit-flavoured sweets.

LICORICE an aniseed-flavoured sweet that comes in straps, tubes and ropes.
allsorts layered sweets consisting of licorice and fondant.
bullets small lengths of licorice coated in chocolate.

LIFESAVERS round hard sweets with a hole in the centre; also known as polo mints.

LOLLIPOP a boiled sweet on a stick.

LOLLY/LOLLIES a confectionery also known as sweets or candy.

MARSHMALLOWS a light, airy sweet that holds its shape. Made from sugar, glucose, gelatine and cornflour.

METAL SPATULA also known as a palette knife. Come in small, medium and large. The larger ones have flexible steel blades. There are two types, straight-bladed, and offset or crank, which is used for getting into tight areas the flat straight blade can't. An excellent tool for icing cakes.

PIPING BAGS
disposable bags made of clear plastic. Discard after each use. Only available in one size and come in packs; available from supermarkets.
paper piping bags made from baking paper (silicone or parchment paper) and discarded after each use. Used for small amounts of icing and writing, etc. See page 113 for directions on making them.
polyester bags are lightweight, flexible and reusable. Wash in hot soapy water after each use and dry, standing over a soft drink bottle. Are available in many different sizes.

READY-MADE ICING also known as ready-to-roll icing (RTR), fondant icing, sugar paste, plastic icing and soft icing. Is sweet tasting, and has a dough-like consistency when kneaded. Is used to cover cakes and make decorations. Roll on a surface dusted lightly with sifted icing sugar or cornflour; don't use too much of either, as the ready-icing will dry and crack when lifted over the cake.

ROLLING PINS come in a variety of sizes; use large ones to roll out the icing, use medium and smaller ones to thin out icing for decorations. They can be made of wood, granite, non-stick plastic, etc.

SPRINKLES coloured cake sprinkles (nonpareils).
chocolate chocolate-flavoured cake sprinkles (vermicelli) or nonpareils.

STYROFOAM tightly-packed polystyrene foam that resists moisture. Available in different-shaped blocks from cake decorating and craft stores.

SUGAR
icing also known as confectioners' sugar or powdered sugar; granulated sugar crushed together with a small amount of added cornflour which stops the sugar from clumping.
pure icing this sugar is also known as confectioners' sugar or powdered sugar, but it has no cornflour added; this means it is very lumpy and it has to be sifted well before use.

INDEX

Published in 2014 by Bauer Media Books

Bauer Media Books is a division of Bauer Media Limited

54 Park St, Sydney

GPO Box 4088, Sydney, NSW 2001.

phone (02) 9282 8618; fax (02) 9126 3702

www.awwcookbooks.com.au

MEDIA GROUP

BAUER MEDIA BOOKS

Publisher - Sally Wright

Editorial and Food Director - Pamela Clark

Director of Sales, Marketing & Rights - Brian Cearnes

Creative Director - Hieu Chi Nguyen

Published and Distributed in the United Kingdom by Octopus Publishing Group

Endeavour House

189 Shaftesbury Avenue

London WC2H 8JY

United Kingdom

phone (+44)(0)207 632 5400; fax (+44)(0)207 632 5405

info@octopus-publishing.co.uk;

www.octopusbooks.co.uk

Printed by Toppan Printing Co., China

International foreign language rights, Brian Cearnes, Bauer Media Books bcearnes@bauer-media.com.au

A catalogue record for this book is available from the British Library.

ISBN: 978 174245 430 6 (paperback)

© Bauer Media Ltd 2014
ABN 18 053 273 546

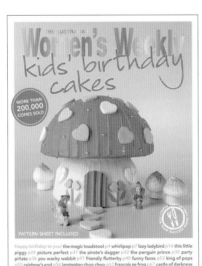

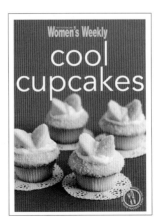